Wedgwood Jasper

Classics, Rarities, & Oddities from Four Centuries

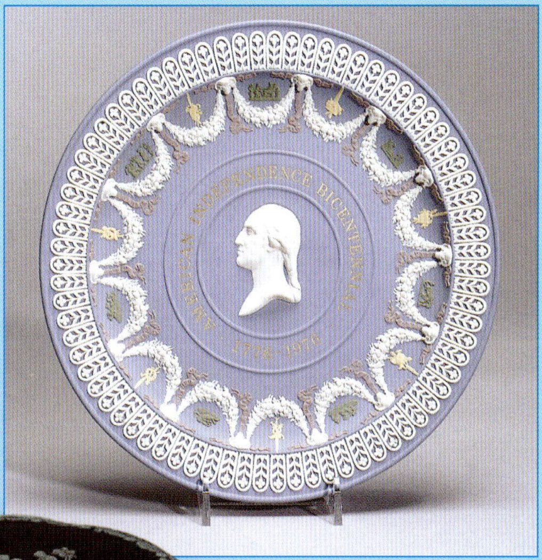

Michael Herman

Schiffer Publishing Ltd®

4880 Lower Valley Road, Atglen, PA 19310 USA

Dedication

With love to my wife, Naomi.

Another Schiffer Book by Michael Herman:

Wedgwood Jasper Ware: A Shape Book and Collectors Guide. ISBN: 0-7643-1926-4. 8 1/2" x 11", 192 pp., 501 color photos. $39.95

Other Schiffer Books on Related Subjects:

Wedgwood Ceramics: Over 200 Years of Innovation and Creativity, Daniel J. Keefe III. ISBN: 0-7643-2298-2. 8 1/2" x 11", 256 pp., 518 color photos. $49.95

Disclaimer

"Wedgwood" and "Jasper" are registered trademarks of Wedgwood Limited, Barlaston, Stoke on Trent, England. There use herein is for identification purposes only. All rights are reserved by their respective owners.

The text and products pictured in this book are from the collection of the author, its publisher, or various private collectors. This book is not sponsored, endorsed or otherwise affiliated with any of the companies whose products are represented herein.

Library of Congress Cataloging-in-Publication Data

Herman, Michael.
Wedgwood jasper : classics, rarities & oddities from four centuries / Michael Herman.
p. cm.
Includes bibliographical references.
ISBN 0-7643-2574-4 (hardcover)
1. Wedgwood ware. 2. Jasperware. 3. Pottery--Collectors and collecting. I. Title.

NK4335.H465 2007
738.0942--dc22
2006023734

Designed by Mark David Bowyer
Type set in Shelley Allegro BT / Souvenir Lt BT

ISBN: 0-7643-2574-4
Printed in China
1 2 3 4

Published by Schiffer Publishing Ltd.
4880 Lower Valley Road
Atglen, PA 19310
Phone: (610) 593-1777; Fax: (610) 593-2002
E-mail: Info@schifferbooks.com

For the largest selection of fine reference books on this and related subjects, please visit our web site at
www.schifferbooks.com
We are always looking for people to write books on new and related subjects. If you have an idea for a book please contact us at the above address.

This book may be purchased from the publisher.
Include $3.95 for shipping.
Please try your bookstore first.
You may write for a free catalog.

In Europe, Schiffer books are distributed by
Bushwood Books
6 Marksbury Ave.
Kew Gardens
Surrey TW9 4JF England
Phone: 44 (0) 20 8392-8585; Fax: 44 (0) 20 8392-9876
E-mail: info@bushwoodbooks.co.uk
Website: www.bushwoodbooks.co.uk
Free postage in the U.K., Europe; air mail at cost.

Contents

Acknowledgments

When I first started to plan this book I knew there were a number of friends that could and would help me fill its pages with photos of superb examples of Wedgwood Jasper from their very special collections. I knew this because they had done so for my previous book on this subject. They are Adele and Alan Barnett, Peggy and Jon Kerner, Elizabeth and Paul Lauer, Marcy Nirschel and Ellen Rubell. This time around they were joined by a group of new friends who opened their homes and collections to my wife and me, toting the unwieldy photography equipment and, in most cases, they even supplied the lunch. These noble souls are: Edward Knowles, David Kroun, Jeffrey Milkins, Dr. and Mrs. Victor Polikoff and Drs. Elaine and Jeffrey Tulman. Three other private collections were opened to my camera but these folks preferred to remain anonymous. Other collectors who supplied pieces for me to shoot were Romaine and Norm Jacobs, Marilyn McClennan, Julie and Lance Pearce and Mary and Pete Rockefeller. Lucie and Bob Reichner kindly supplied me with some photos from their personal collection as did an English friend, Sarah Marie White.

Another wonderful source for photos of Wedgwood Jasper pieces is located at the Sands Point Preserve in Sands Point, New York. For now, at least, three important Wedgwood collections are housed at this location. They are the Buten Collection of Wedgwood, the Donald and Marsha Levine Ceramics and Glass Collection and the Esme Wedgwood Collection. Gary Hammond, the Museum Registrar, gave me unlimited access to these collections as well as to the indispensable Buten Library on the premises. I owe him a great amount of thanks for his unstinting support and cooperation.

An additional round of thanks is due to Lynn Miller, Information Officer at the Wedgwood Museum in Barlaston, England, who not only sent me several photos but also always stood ready to authoritatively answer any questions that I needed answering.

A large number of photos of very special pieces of Wedgwood Jasper that are found in this book are here because of the help of two members of the staff of Skinner, Inc. of Boston and Bolton, Massachusetts. Anne Trodella, Skinner's Public Relations Coordinator was always ready to quickly supply me with any photo I requested from Skinner's vast archive. Stuart Slavid, the head of Skinner's Ceramics Department (and frequently seen appraiser on PBS's *Antiques Road Show*) pointed me in Anne Trodella's direction and also supplied me with a number of important photos. I am very grateful to both of them.

Other commercial organizations that contributed photos used herein are Leo Kaplan, Inc. of New York City, Shapiro Auctioneers of Sydney, Australia, Stamford Auctions of Stamford, Connecticut, and Terry Rodgers and Melody Jewelers of New York City.

Thanks go also to my editor at Schiffer Publishing, Douglas Congdon-Martin for allowing me to borrow the company photography equipment whenever I requested it, helping me improve my photographic skills and giving me much encouragement every time I showed him my work.

Finally, let me thank the most important of my collaborators, my wife Naomi, who was my recording secretary through all the photo shoots from Connecticut to Virginia and a perfect companion at these and all other times.

1. Introduction

My previous book, *Wedgwood Jasper Ware, A Shape Book and Collectors' Guide*, was written and published in 2003. Its main purpose was to be a reference tool for beginning and intermediate Wedgwood Jasper collectors to help them identify and learn more about the various items that they already possessed or planned to add to their collections. That book had limited itself basically to one type of Wedgwood Jasper production, namely dipped Jasper that had been manufactured primarily in the period between the middle of the nineteenth century to the end of its run in the early years of the Second World War (c.1939-1941). The reason for that focus was simple — that was what I collected and what I knew best to write about. The photos shown in that book came from the collections of the author, several close friends as well as a local museum.

The current book has cast a much wider net and attempts to document through pictures the entire history of Wedgwood Jasper from its early production in the late eighteenth century to examples produced in the initial years of our twenty-first century. When the publisher requested a second Wedgwood book from me I was somewhat at a loss, at first, to know what to do. I knew my first book covered only a small part of the vast Wedgwood Jasper panoply. However, I wondered where I could obtain enough additional photos over a much broader range to fill another volume. The problem was soon solved as the success and wide dissemination of my first book opened many new doors for me. I was invited to talk about my book at meetings of the Wedgwood Societies of New York, Boston and Washington, D.C., as well as the Wedgwood International Seminar's meeting in Birmingham, Alabama. As a result, I have been able to visit and photograph the contents of some of the most prestigious and comprehensive Wedgwood Jasper collections in the northeast United States as well as to obtain superb photos from various auction houses. Whereas my first book was basically a "blue Jasper" book (reflecting my own collection) the current book can easily be called the "rainbow" Jasper book as I have attempted to include a plethora of pieces in every color and combinations of colors that the Wedgwood Company ever baked in a kiln.

Once again, the main purpose of this book is the identification of Wedgwood Jasper products for the education and delight of the collector. Though this book has been thoroughly researched, no scholarly insights are promised or delivered. That was not my purpose. While I mainly concentrated in my first book on the types of pieces more readily available and affordable by the average collector this book includes many more pieces that could be called "museum quality" with prices to match. Hopefully some of my readers will not be daunted by such astronomic values and will bear in mind that the author is completely empathetic and shares their fantasies. As before, however, complete comprehensiveness is an unobtainable goal as Wedgwood Jasper has been produced in such a variety of shapes, styles, and colors over the course of the last two and a half centuries.

The structure of this book is similar to its predecessor. After several brief introductory essays the bulk of the work consists of a photo gallery of Wedgwood Jasper shapes classified by type and annotated with descriptive information about each piece. I truly hope that my second Wedgwood Jasper Ware book will prove as useful and enjoyable as my original survey of this ever-fascinating subject.

2. Wedgwood Jasper from the Eighteenth to the Twenty-First Centuries

Josiah Wedgwood (1730-1795) founded the company that still bears his name in 1759. He came from a family that had been potters for three generations preceding him. His company produced a variety of products in different types of bodies. He constantly innovated, improving upon the materials and methods that were the stock in trade of the industry that he was born into.

Jasper was Josiah Wedgwood's most important creation in that it was a completely new ceramic body. After a number of years, starting in 1771, that saw thousands of experiments and frustrations the new product was perfected in 1774 and introduced to the public in 1775. Wedgwood had struggled to invent this new formulation for a very specific reason. As a shrewd entrepreneur he knew there was money to be made in the great interest in classical subjects engendered by the uncovering of the volcano-buried Roman cities of Pompeii and Herculaneum. The burgeoning middle classes wanted to own ancient artifacts. However, there were not enough to go around and most people could not afford them in any case. So a market for copies, reproductions and other classical looking objects was out there and Wedgwood wanted a ceramic body that could simulate these ancient treasures that were often characterized by figures in bas-relief. Another strong influence at this time was the work of the architect Robert Adam (1728-1792) who painted interiors with white figures over a pastel colored background. In all the experimentation Wedgwood was seeking to create a body that would come out white after firing and would not require a glaze. Color and relief could then be applied and then the product would be fired a second time. The result was the familiar object we know today with its cameo boldly jutting out from a matte surface. At first Jasper was used basically for smaller objects such as cameos and intaglios that could be set for jewelry. However, before too much time had passed, Jasper's use was expanded to include a variety of larger objects including vases, bowls, and déjeuner sets

Jasper is a type of stoneware given this name by Wedgwood as it resembled a naturally occurring variety of quartz. To this day Jasper is a registered trademark of the Wedgwood Company. Over the centuries it has proven to be the most popular and recognizable of Wedgwood's many products. Almost from the very beginning there were two basic types of Jasper, solid and dip. In solid Jasper the coloring agent is blended into the mixture before firing, whereas with Jasper dip the color is applied on the surface of an object that has already been fired and then is fired again. The latter type was obviously more economical as less of the very costly coloring material had to be used. It is easy to differentiate the two basic Jasper types as one can readily see the original base color (usually but not always white) on the bottom, back, or inside of the object. Colors used by Wedgwood in this early period included several shades of blue as well as green, black, white, brown, yellow, buff, gray and lilac. Items could also receive more than one dip color and, while tricolor Jasper dip pieces are the most common, there are also objects found with four and five colors. Furthermore, by use of an engine-turning lathe, elaborate color patterns such as diceware and strapware could be produced.

Solid Jasper. Bowl (Footed), pale blue, *"Boys at Play,"* mark: WEDGWOOD, ca. 1790, 5" x 9". *Anonymous Private Collection.* $3500-4000.

Jasper Dip. Wine Cooler, dark blue, *"Urania,"* mark: WEDGWOOD, ca. 1890, 5.25" x 5.25". *Author's Collection.* $300-400.

Tricolor. Vase (Dancing Hours – 275) on Base, black and yellow (dip), mark: WEDGWOOD, ENGLAND, ca. 1900, 9" x 4". *Courtesy of the Kerner Collection.* $1500-1800.

Four-Color. Vase (58), dark blue, sage green, and lilac (dip), "Sacrifice to Hymen," ca. 1850, 11.5" x 4.5". *Courtesy of Edward L. Knowles.* $4000-5000.

Diceware. Cup and Saucer, diceware lilac (dip, with green quatrefoils and lapidary polished interior), mark: WEDGWOOD 3, ca. 1790, 2.25" x 2.75". *Courtesy of Ellen Rubell.* $1500-2000.

Strapware. Bowl, , strapware white (dip, with applied sage green and yellow strapwork), mark: WEDGWOOD, ca. 1790, 4.5" x 9". *Courtesy of Jeffrey S. Milkins.* $4000-5000.

Wedgwood spared no effort to make his products truly outstanding and gathered around him a galaxy of well known and highly skilled artists who created the bas-relief designs that became the most prominent feature of Jasper products. Chief among these artists were the modelers John Flaxman Sr. (1726-1795), John Flaxman Jr. (1755-1826) and William Hackwood (c.1757-1839), the painter George Stubbs (1724-1806), noted for his horses, and the designers Lady Elizabeth Templetown (1747-1823) and Lady Diana Beauclerk (1734-1808). Other artists included Henry Webber (1754-1826), John Charles Lochée (1751-c.1791), and Joachim Smith (d. 1803). These artists usually worked anonymously for Wedgwood and their creations became the property of the Factory. The Flaxmans and Hackwood produced numerous designs based on classical mythology that appeared on medallions, plaques, and standing objects. Lady Templetown usually specialized in more contemporary and workaday subjects such as the Domestic Employment series, whereas Lady Beauclerk's subjects were most often cherubic looking boys at play. Their work can truly be called Wedgwood "classics" because, though first produced in the eighteenth century, the purchaser or collector of twenty-first century Wedgwood Jasper items will find many of these designs still current.

Lady Elizabeth Templetown. Tea Canister, pale blue (solid), *"Domestic Employment,"* mark: WEDGWOOD, ca. 1790, 6" x 3.5". *Courtesy of the Kerner Collection.* $1200-1500.

Lady Diana Beauclerk. Jug (Club), medium blue (dip), *"Bacchanalian Boys at Play,"* mark: WEDGWOOD, ca. 1820, 7.5" x 6.25". *Courtesy of Edward L. Knowles.* $1500-1800.

John Flaxman Jr. Vase (298), lilac (solid), *"Hercules in the Garden of the Hesperides,"* mark: WEDGWOOD, MADE IN ENGLAND, 1960, 13" x 7". *Anonymous Private Collection.* $900-1000.

After Josiah Wedgwood's death in 1795, Jasper of very high quality continued to be produced into the next century. As time passed, however, an inevitable change of fashion took place. The declining interest in Neo-classical patterns that had already begun in the last years of the eighteenth century became quite rapid after 1810. The introduction of new colors and shapes did not improve matters significantly and the use of Jasper for larger items was almost totally abandoned by the 1820s. The situation was exacerbated by the fact that Wedgwood's original formula for Jasper had been lost. It was at this stage that the Jasper body was basically replaced with a more cost-effective (and coarser) stoneware body that was used as the base for the now predominant Jasper dip. Having been discontinued between 1829 and 1860 solid Jasper was reintroduced in 1860 on a very limited basis, though Jasper dip would continue to be the overwhelmingly utilized type until World War II. By the 1870's Jasper production, both dip and solid was back in full swing. Reproductions of items from the first Josiah's time as well as many new interesting shapes and colors were being turned out. Modelers who created important new bas-relief designs in Jasper for the Wedgwood Company during this period include Frederick Schenck (1849-1908) and Charles Toft (1831-1909). A new color, unique to this period was a turquoise dip that was produced between 1875 and 1885.Although many fine pieces were produced in the late nineteenth century there seems to be a consensus that the quality of the items never duplicated the work done a century earlier.

Charles Toft. Vase (372), sage green (dip), *"Dancing Ladies and Girls,"* mark: WEDGWOOD, ca. 1880 (modeled by Charles Toft), 13.25" h. *Courtesy of Skinner, Inc., Boston and Bolton, Ma.* $1200-1500.

Turquoise. Cup and Saucer, (dip), *"Sacrifice Figures,"* mark: WEDGWOOD, ca. 1875, 2.5" x 5.5". *Courtesy of Dr. and Mrs. Victor Polikoff.* $1000-1200.

The history of Wedgwood Jasper from the beginning of the twentieth century until World War II is basically a continuation of developments started in the late nineteenth century. More and more of the items in the Jasper production were geared to useful wares that could be employed for mundane purposes in homes and gardens and could make more money for the Company. Wedgwood started calling this type of Jasper dip product "Bas-Relief Ware." Both the material used and most of the shapes utilized were not new. As before, the Jasper dip was applied to a stoneware body and, as always, the white ornaments were applied to the surface. As already mentioned, items made in this line were generally produced for use rather than display. As products were made for domestic use, tea sets, tobacco jars, cruet sets, jugs, bowls, etc. were usually glazed to protect their porous interior surfaces. Nearly all the dip pieces that were made in the early twentieth century are from the Bas-Relief Ware line. However, a smaller line made completely of Jasper continued to be produced. This more expensive method was reserved for the most prestigious pieces such as Dancing Hours bowls and Trophy plates that could command much higher prices. It is often hard to tell the difference between the two lines especially when the Bas-Relief pieces are extremely well made. On the whole, however, the totally jasper pieces tend to have a smoother feel as the stoneware used in Bas-Relief Ware is a somewhat rougher material.

Bas Relief Ware. Coffee Set (129), dark blue (dip), *"Sacrifice Figures,"* marks: WEDGWOOD, ca. 1890, 7.5" x 8.5" (coffee pot), 5" x 4.75" (sugar), 2.5" x 3" (creamer). *Author's Collection.* $600-700 (for the set).

Jasper Only. Trophy Plate, tricolor (dip, black with yellow quatrefoils), *"Aurora,"* mark: WEDGWOOD, MADE IN ENGLAND, 1978, 9" diameter. *Courtesy of the Kerner Collection.* $1000-1200.

The early years of the twentieth century can easily be characterized as the era of Harry Barnard and Bert Bentley. Barnard (1862-1933) introduced many new shapes and styles in Jasper. A notable example of his work is a style called "sgraffito" in which a design is cut through the layer of Jasper color to expose the white body that lies underneath. Bentley (1878-1937) was the Wedgwood Factory's Master Potter. He introduced new designs that appeared on plaques as well as a new issue of the Portland Vase. The Barnard and Bentley period also saw the introduction of new colors in Jasper dip. The most prominent was crimson, first introduced experimentally in 1910 and then put into general production between 1929 and 1935. Splendid color that it was, its history was truncated as the problem of the crimson color running into the white bas-reliefs could never be totally overcome thus making its production uneconomical. As so much that came out of the kiln had to be discarded the surviving pieces became somewhat scarce and would so transform crimson as the most desirable of colors among latter-day Wedgwood Jasper collectors. Other new colors introduced at this time were olive green (that suffered the same bleeding problem as crimson) and a yellow buff that was ornamented with black bas-reliefs.

Crimson. Teapot (146),(dip), *"Sacrifice Figures,"* mark: WEDGWOOD, ENGLAND, ca. 1925. 6" x 10". *Courtesy of Elizabeth and Paul Lauer.* $1200-1500.

Harry Barnard. Jug (Dutch), dark blue (dip, sgraffito, signed by Harry Barnard), mark: WEDGWOOD, ENGLAND, ca. 1895, 4.75" x 5". *Courtesy of the Buten Collection of Wedgwood at the Sands Point Preserve, Sands Point, N.Y.* $1200-1500.

Yellow Buff and Black. Vase, (dip), mark: WEDGWOOD, ca. 1930, 9.75" x 5.5". *Courtesy of the Donald and Marsha Levine Ceramics and Glass Collection at the Sands Point Preserve, Sands Point, N.Y.* $3000-5000.

Olive Green. Jardinière (317), (dip), *"Muses,"* mark: WEDGWOOD, ENGLAND, ca. 1910, 9" x 10.25". *Courtesy of Elizabeth and Paul Lauer.* $800-1000.

The early twentieth century also saw the addition of two other lines of Wedgwood Jasper. The first of these was called "Mounting Ware." This was quite an extensive line of useful wares characterized by metal bands around their rims, often with metal covers and, sometimes, metal handles as well. The most popular Mounting Ware items were salad bowls, biscuit barrels, cruet sets and marmalade jars. Many of the Mounting Ware shapes were also found in the regular Bas-Relief line, but the majority of these shapes were only offered as Mounting Ware. Another separate Wedgwood Jasper line was known as "Arms Ware." Arms Ware items were usually sold in souvenir shops around Britain and the British Empire and displayed the civic, national, or colonial coat of arms of the place where they were sold. Most of the pieces offered in this line were very small plates, jugs, vases, etc. Some Arms Ware shapes were unique to this line while others could be the more common shapes in which the usual Neo-classical bas-reliefs have been replaced by the appropriate arms. Both the Mounting Ware and Arms Ware lines were produced exclusively in Jasper dip and neither line was characterized by very high quality.

World War II would prove to be a major watershed in the history of Wedgwood Jasper. The production of Jas-

Mounting Ware. Biscuit Barrel, dark blue (dip, with silver plated mount and handle), *"Offering to Peace,"* mark: WEDGWOOD, ENGLAND, ca. 1900, 6" x 5.75". *Courtesy of the Kerner Collection.* $500-600.

Arms Ware. Vase (Miniature), dark blue (dip), *"Arms of Birmingham,"* mark: WEDGWOOD, ENGLAND, ca. 1900, 3" x 1.5". *Author's Collection.* $200-300.

per and most other decorative ceramics basically ground to a halt in 1941 as wartime contingencies mandated that manufacturers had to concentrate on utilitarian products for domestic and military requirements. Furthermore, when the Wedgwood Company opened its new factory at Barlaston there was no provision for the manufacture of Jasper products until 1948, when the move from the old factory at Etruria to the new facilities was completed. At that time an entirely new formulation for Jasper was introduced. The inventor of the "new" Jasper was Norman Wilson (1902-1988), master potter and ceramics designer who was Wedgwood's production director from 1946 to 1961. This is the type of Jasper still in use today, with a surface texture that has an entirely different feel than its predecessor, being somewhat rougher to the touch. The postwar Jasper production is almost always solid rather than dip, with the latter type used rarely for prestige items.

For general production items the colors most utilized were pale blue, sage green and black. Dark or cobalt blue (as it is popularly known), so familiar and predominant in the prewar period was not revived, but was eventually replaced by two new dark blue shades known as Royal and Portland Blue in 1953 and 1980 respectively. Other solid colors introduced or brought back in the last decades of the twentieth century and put into general production included terracotta (1957), lilac (1960), primrose yellow (1976), pink (1982), teal (1984), taupe (1984), and grey (1991). Some of these modern colors were quite ephemeral and were offered to the public only briefly, while terracotta and, especially, lilac had much longer life spans. There were other colors that were formulated for specific commemorative purposes and were not used otherwise. The twenty-first century saw the introduction of a new red Jasper color called "wine." It somewhat resembles crimson and no doubt Wedgwood was attempting to satisfy the cravings of frustrated crimson collectors who could not find or could not afford the classic color of the previous century.

Royal Blue. Vase (Oak Leaf), (dip), *"Psyche Bound to a Tree,"* mark: WEDGWOOD®, MADE IN ENGLAND, 1988, 5.75" x 3.5". *Courtesy of Adele Ierubino Barnett.* $300-400.

Portland Blue. Custard Cup, (solid), mark: WEDGWOOD, MADE IN ENGLAND, 2001, 3" x 2.75". *Courtesy of David Kroun.* $200-300.

Modern Wedgwood Colors. Group of Trays and Plates, (all solid): Lloyd's of London green, taupe, primrose, pink, terra cotta, teal and cane, marks: WEDGWOOD, MADE IN ENGLAND, ca. 1950s through 1980s, various sizes. *Courtesy of Alan Barnett.* Various prices.

Wine. Spill vase, (solid), mark: WEDGWOOD, MADE IN ENGLAND, 2003, 4" x 2.5". *Courtesy of Adele Ierubino Barnett.* $100-200.

The vast majority of Jasper production from its post World War II revival to the present has been the familiar array of trays, jugs, vases, etc. (mostly in pale blue) that even the most casual observer instantly recognizes as Wedgwood. Within this range one finds the omnipresent Christmas plates and jugs as well as other annually issued holiday series. Additional Jasper series in this period included the Prunus and Symmetry Collections as well as a series devoted to the American Bicentennial (1976). Commemoratives devoted to the Royal Family were also issued with great regularity.

An additional source for collectors of Wedgwood Jasper was the Wedgwood Collectors Society. This American based organization that began operations about 1970 and lasted into the next decade offered numerous items available exclusively from the Society and produced in limited quantities in Jasper as well as in Basalt and Queen's Ware. Of particular interest to Jasper collectors were items issued in unusual color combinations. Series, such as those mentioned above, as well as the Society pieces have been very popular with general Jasper collectors, but the Wedgwood Company has also tried to appeal to collectors with more aesthetic tastes (and deeper pockets) by producing prestige items in more limited quantities and of much higher quality. These included reproductions of classic Wedgwood shapes and designs from earlier centuries. Examples included a series of pieces in diceware patterns, as well as some classic vase shapes originally produced in the days of the first Josiah Wedgwood. Straddling the two types of series mentioned above was the Egyptian Collection of 1978 that included both an extremely limited run of superbly crafted reproductions of Wedgwood's early nineteenth century Canopic Vases and a number of smaller items for the general collecting market issued in much larger quantities.

Prunus Collection. Bowl, primrose (solid), mark: WEDGWOOD, MADE IN ENGLAND, 1978 3.5" x 8". *Courtesy of the Kerner Collection.* $250-350.

Wedgwood Collectors Society. Bridge Set, white (solid, with relief in taupe, yellow, terra cotta and sage green), mark: WEDGWOOD MADE IN ENGLAND, 1979 and stamped in gold WEDGWOOD COLLECTORS SOCIETY,, various sizes, *Courtesy of David Kroun.* $500-600.

Symmetry Collection. Two Vases and a Box, pale blue (dip), mark: WEDGWOOD®, MADE IN ENGLAND, ca.1989, 6.75" x 3.75" and 5" x 3.5 (vases), 3.25" x 3.5" (box). *Courtesy of Adele Ierubino Barnett* . $500-600 for the set.

Prestige Limited Edition. Vase (Athena), diceware (dip, royal blue and sage green with sage green quatrefoils), *"Aurora,"* mark: WEDGWOOD, MADE IN ENGLAND, 1976 (limited edition of 200 from 'Wedgwood Masterpiece Series'), 9.5" x 4.5". *Courtesy of the Kerner Collection.* $1500-1800.

Egyptian Collection. Canopic Vase, black (solid, with terracotta relief), mark: WEDGWOOD, MADE IN ENGLAND, 1978, 9.375" h. ". *Courtesy of Skinner, Inc., Boston and Bolton, Ma.* $1200-1500.

Summing up we can easily determine that Wedgwood Jasper's greatest days were in the past. Despite past rumors about its imminent demise, Wedgwood Jasper is still with us in the twenty-first century. Should you find yourself in the various Waterford Wedgwood shops in the United States or United Kingdom you will be able to purchase the limited selection of shapes and colors still on offer as well as a few prestige items on display in separate showcases. Wedgwood Jasper has had a glorious history and it seems that the many collectors and admirers of this unique and superb type of ceramic body will project this history well into the future.

3. Wedgwood Marks and Dating Wedgwood Jasper

One of Josiah Wedgwood's greatest innovations had little to do with ceramics at all. By marking his products with the company name he actually invented what we now call the "brand name." An extremely important aspect of Wedgwood Jasper collecting is knowledge about the meaning of the incised marks that are found on practically every piece. However, unmarked Wedgwood pieces do exist and certain types of items, such as perfume bottles, are hardly ever found with marks. Yet a general rule of thumb would be that if an item does not have a clearly readable Wedgwood mark it is not Wedgwood.

The main reason to learn these marks is for the purpose of approximately (in most cases) dating the pieces in your collection. The familiar, all capitals, incised **WEDGWOOD** mark was used from the very beginning of Jasper production. Less frequently seen marks used in the eighteenth century include various forms of **WEDGWOOD & BENTLEY** as well as an upper and lower case **Wedgwood**. Once we go beyond the earliest period, the simple **WEDGWOOD** mark stands alone until the last decade of the nineteenth century. In 1891 a very protectionist United States government passed the McKinley Tariff Act that required all imported goods to indicate their country of origin. Naturally, as Wedgwood had a very sizable market on this side of the Atlantic, the factory quickly complied with this regulation. Thus **ENGLAND** began to be incised along with **WEDGWOOD** usually on opposite ends of a piece's underside. Also found in this period are some pieces incised **ETRURIA** in addition to the other marks. **MADE IN ENGLAND** was introduced around 1898 but did not come into general use for another ten years. The only other important modification of the mark took place in 1929 when a new type face known as sans serif was introduced. The new **WEDGWOOD** mark had a more contemporary look but did not completely replace its predecessor and the two marks have coexisted down to our own time.

So what follows are some very general guidelines, which are probably correct most of the time. Pieces incised **WEDGWOOD** only usually pre-date 1891 while those marked **WEDGWOOD ENGLAND (ETRURIA)** date from about 1891 to 1908. **WEDGWOOD, MADE IN ENGLAND** usually indicates manufacture from about 1908 forward and the sans-serif **WEDGWOOD, MADE IN ENGLAND** mark means the piece can be no earlier than 1929. Bear in mind, however, that many pieces marked only **WEDGWOOD** are not necessarily of pre-twentieth century vintage. Such pieces may have been produced only for domestic or Empire markets making compliance with American law unnecessary.

While the above information about dating Wedgwood Jasper is usually consistent and general, what follows is more specific though exceedingly inconsistent. From 1860 to 1929 a system of impressed date codes was used on various Wedgwood earthenware bodies. Unfortunately, for our purposes, it was used quite infrequently for Jasper. However, when the code does appear it gives a collector the best possible chance to specifically date an item from the period under discussion. From 1860 to 1906 the code consisted of three letters impressed one after the other (e.g., **TWR**). The first letter indicated the month while the second was a potter's mark. Most important was the third letter that indicated the year. The year letter series started in 1860 with **O** and continued alphabetically to **Z** for the year 1871. In 1872 a new cycle began with **A** and transversed the entire alphabet until it reached **Z** in 1897. A final three-letter cycle then began in 1898 with **A** and ceased in 1906 with **I**. In 1907 the alphabet letter for the year continued with **J** but the first letter of the code was replaced with the number **3**; this system continued until the letter **Z** was reached in 1923. Finally a new alphabetic cycle commenced in 1924 with a **4** replacing the **3**. This ultimate series went from **A** to **F** and concluded in 1929.

Besides its infrequency of use, the three letter code used between 1860 and 1906 had an additional drawback in that every year letter, with the exceptions of **J** through **N,** was used twice. If the letter code is accompanied with **WEDGWOOD ENGLAND** or **WEDGWOOD, MADE IN ENGLAND** there is a good chance that the actual year is indicated since we know the pieces were probably made after 1891. Similarly the absence of these marks may tell us that the pieces belong to the earlier year cycle. However if we see a year letter such as **R** how do we know which year it stands for, 1863 or 1889? We really cannot be sure. The Wedgwood mark evidence does not help us for the letters **O** through **T** so the pieces can be dated either 1860 to 1865 or 1886 to 1891. The following chart extracted from Robin Reilly's *Wedgwood,*

The Illustrated Dictionary shows the years that the third letter of a three-letter mark could represent:

A		1872	1898
B		1873	1899
C		1874	1900
D		1875	1901
E		1876	1902
F		1877	1903
G		1878	1904
H		1879	1905
I		1880	1906
J		1881	
K		1882	
L		1883	
M		1884	
N		1885	
O	1860	1886	
P	1861	1887	
Q	1862	1888	
R	1863	1889	
S	1864	1890	
T	1865	1891	
U	1866	1892	
V	1867	1893	
W	1868	1894	
X	1869	1895	
Y	1870	1896	
Z	1871	1897	

In the last decade of general production of Wedgwood Jasper at the Barlaston factory (c.1930-1940), it is possible to find a piece with an actual date mark impressed. The year is so indicated by its last two numbers (i.e., **35** = 1935). Like the codes mentioned above finding pieces with such a date mark is a very rare occurrence. Similarly a pair of curved dashes, popularly known as "mustache marks," can be found very occasionally on Jasper pieces. Such marks place the piece in the first two decades of the nineteenth century.

The marks found on post-World War II Jasper products are the basic **WEDGWOOD**, **MADE IN ENGLAND** usually, though not always, in san serif style. Date marks represented by the last two numerals of the year were employed pretty consistently from the 1950s through the 1980s. After this time date marks appear occasionally, but now one usually finds an incised registry mark ® next to the company name.

There are other numerical marks that are found on Jasper pieces but these serve functions other than dating. For example, there can be found marks such as **2½** or **3½** that tell us the size in inches of a piece (usually its height). However, a more commonly found size indicator for late nineteenth and twentieth century pieces is a series of numbers that are all multiples of six. These numbers indicate the number of pieces that could fit on a shelf in the kiln. Thus the largest pieces are marked with a **6**, while the number increases to the smallest pieces that are incised with a **54**. Additional number groupings, such as **953** and **1012** indicate a Wedgwood factory-designated shape number of a particular piece (usually a vase).

The last thing to be said about Wedgwood marks is a word of caution. Should one come across a piece of Jasper marked **WEDGWOOD & CO.** or **WEDGWOOD & CO., LTD**. be advised that such pieces were not made by Josiah Wedgwood and Sons.

4. Collecting Wedgwood Jasper

Like most other hobbies, collecting Wedgwood Jasper is quite an individual endeavor and passion. No two collections are the same and many are totally dissimilar. In preparing this book and its predecessor, I have seen many Wedgwood collections. Very few collections are exclusively Jasper or even exclusively Wedgwood as they contain either other Wedgwood types or the products of Wedgwood's competitors.

What one collects has to do with three factors: taste, display space, and, above all, finances. Some collectors concentrate on different periods depending on these factors. I have visited collections that consisted almost totally of pieces from the eighteenth century as well as others that had very few items made earlier than World War II. Certain collections concentrate on one color of Jasper, while others may lean towards a particular decorative pattern such as Muses or Dancing Hours figures. Yet, in general, it seems that most Wedgwood collectors opt for eclecticism either initially or eventually. However, no matter what is collected the passionate collector almost always presents his or her treasures with curatorial perfection. The Wedgwood pieces are displayed in curio cabinets, open shelves, on pedestals and wherever else they can be lovingly viewed and safe from passing elbows and other body parts. When space is at a premium such as in an apartment like the author's, plastic risers and other bases can readily turn one shelf into several levels.

Wedgwood collectors usually seek the company of others who share their interest, as their own family and usual friends often look at this passion as an odd way to spend so much time and money. Fortunately there are organizations to give comfort to these "lost souls." They are called Wedgwood Societies and in the U.S.A. they exist in several large urban areas such as New York, Washington D.C., Boston, and Southern California. Their purpose is to bring Wedgwood collectors together, supply them with information via newsletters and meetings and to further their Wedgwood education by sponsoring lectures by leading experts in the field and authors of Wedgwood books. They charge a very reasonable membership fee and their individual aims, schedules and locations can easily be found on the internet.

Following upon what was just said, the kind of information most avidly sought by Wedgwood collectors is how to add additional pieces to one's collection. As someone who began collecting Wedgwood Jasper only a little more than ten years ago, I can easily state that many things have changed for collectors over that decade. Most of those changes can be attributed to one phenomenon: eBay, the online auction megasite. When my wife and I embarked on our Wedgwood hobby in the mid-90s, Wedgwood Jasper pieces could be found in substantial quantities in antique malls, at antique shows, and even in some smallish antique shops. Naturally, more modern pieces from the 1950s through the 1980s predominated the offerings. However, older Jasper could also be regularly found.

Today much of the interesting Wedgwood once found in the above venues has migrated to eBay and other online sites. On any typical day eBay offers between seven and ten thousand Wedgwood items of all types, of which around twenty percent are usually Jasper. The vast majority of the Jasper offers are, of course, the more recent products but that still leaves a sizable number of pre-World War II pieces as well. Thus the entire gamut of Wedgwood Jasper, from the earliest days (very rarely) to items produced in the current year, can be seen and purchased, if you are lucky enough to place the winning bid. The more common pieces including many less-than-rare antiques can be purchased at bargain prices. However, when unusual items are offered the prices can often skyrocket, especially if two or more bidders were determined to end up on top.

Antique shows (known as antique fairs in the United Kingdom), though not as fruitful a source of Wedgwood Jasper as they once were, can still be a great place to find a special piece. This is especially true of the larger shows where hundreds of dealers are represented making the odds higher that at least some of them will have some interesting Wedgwood to sell. Despite the fact that a number of Wedgwood specialist dealers no longer appear at these shows (having opted out for the less strenuous and, perhaps, more profitable world of cyberspace), a collector still may do well at one of these shows on a good day. A few Wedgwood specialist dealers are still out there and some still do appear at various shows, especially at the Baltimore Summer Antiques Fair held annually around Labor Day. Other good antique shows in the Northeast are the Triple Piers Show in New York

City and the Atlantique City show in Atlantic City, New Jersey, that are both semi-annual events. Prices tend to be quite high at shows, but if you find a piece that you really want and can afford it, you just write a check for the dealer and do not have to worry about someone coming along and outbidding you, as can often happen on eBay and other auction situations.

This leads directly to the old fashioned type of auction that existed before the age of the internet, and, despite eBay is still thriving today. As far as Wedgwood collectors are concerned the most important auction house in the United States is Skinner, Inc. of Boston and Bolton, Massachusetts. Usually twice a year, Skinner offers a vast array of quality Wedgwood that draws a sizable attendance from across the country as well as across the Atlantic. Beautiful catalogs are produced that illustrate the many superb pieces on offer. Once again, prices tend to move quite high as there are a lot of collectors and dealers competing for these treasures. Furthermore, as these same lots are now appearing simultaneously on eBay the competition is now even greater than before.

Finally, another good source for collecting Wedgwood Jasper is the Mother Country of Wedgwood itself. It is often said that more Wedgwood is found in America than in the United Kingdom these days. As someone who travels to London at least once a year, I find that claim highly exaggerated. It is always a treat to go to Portobello Road in West London on a Saturday morning to explore the seemingly endless arcades of antique dealers displaying their wares. While some visits have been more productive than others we have yet to leave that market without acquiring some interesting piece of Wedgwood Jasper either from the several specialist dealers or from a generalist dealer who just happened to have an item we could not live without. Other antique markets in London have a lot less to offer, but one can always get lucky as we have on several occasions. With the declining U.S. dollar of recent years prices for good Wedgwood can be more prohibitive than in the past but I have found that one can as easily find a bargain there as here.

5. The Photo Gallery of Wedgwood Jasper

Gathered here is a large display of photos of Wedgwood Jasper pieces that have been classified into a number of categories. Every category is introduced by a brief paragraph that discusses its contents. Most of the pertinent information about each piece will be found in the accompanying caption and, hopefully, the caption and the photo will between them satisfy the reader's curiosity about any item shown.

A Note on Captions

In the pages that follow you will find captioned photos that will illustrate the great variety of Wedgwood Jasper that may be found by collectors. What is shown in this or any other book about Wedgwood only scratches the surface as numberless other types may be found as well. Wedgwood has produced and is still producing a staggering variety in Jasper, alone, over the last two and a half centuries. This is what the author has tracked down and you will have to forgive him if your favorite pieces or types do not appear here. Some large categories of Wedgwood Jasper, such as portrait medallions, are barely touched, while others, such as thimbles or the very popular Beatrix Potter series, make no appearance at all, as they were not available for me to photograph. The captions will tell you the basic information about each piece that is illustrated. These include the name and/or number of the piece (if known), the color or colors, solid or dip, the mark(s), the size, age, and value. The names and numbers are derived from various Wedgwood Factory shape books or other Wedgwood reference books. Measurements are, for the most part, expressed as height by width unless otherwise specified. When I personally could measure items I could give more complete measurements. In most cases the age is an approximation based on marks and other clues. When the word "tricolor" is used it should be assumed that white is included among the three colors even if not specifically stated. In addition, I have given the name, when known, of the bas-reliefs (in quotation marks) that are most prominently displayed on the piece. Also found in the captions are the names of the persons or institutions in whose collections the pieces are either found or from whence the photo was obtained.

A Note on Price Ranges

Always a tricky and imperfect business, the price ranges listed for the Wedgwood Jasper pieces displayed in this book have been determined in several ways. Most of the items are not owned by the author so I asked the actual owners to give me an estimate of what they assumed their pieces were worth based on what they had paid and taking into account that many were purchased years ago and are now worth somewhat more. A somewhat different formula was used for the large number of photos that were supplied by several auction houses. In these cases I based the values on the selling price realized at auction often modified by certain factors including the passage of years since the auctions took place and by treating most items as if they were in good to excellent condition even if they were not sold this way originally. In general, however, Wedgwood Jasper prices are determined by several criteria. These include age, condition, quality, size, color, marks, provenance, and rarity.

Even after all these variables are taken into account the price you will pay for any piece of Wedgwood Jasper (except current items sold in Waterford Wedgwood stores or other retail establishments) is what you are willing to pay (especially at an auction) and what the dealer is willing to sell it for. This situation is manifestly reflected when two similar items are listed here with, at times, quite divergent price ranges. As the Wedgwood items shown in this book run almost the entire gamut between the inexpensive to the priceless the major purpose of the prices is to establish a kind of relativity of value. In short, use the price ranges as rough guides only.

I. Some Special Wedgwood Jasper Collectibles

As a kind of an appetizer to a much larger main course, the Gallery begins with a few categories of Wedgwood Jasper that have proved very collectible over the years. They cover a broad range of rarity and cost. While some groups go as far back as the eighteenth century, others are strictly products of the twentieth. In all cases, other examples of these types of Wedgwood Jasper will be found among the Gallery of Shapes in the next section.

a. Diceware

Diceware is a special type of multicolored Wedgwood Jasper. It was first produced in 1785 and is a prime example of Wedgwood's creative use of the engine-turning lathe. As a type of Jasper dip, the diced pattern is produced when the lathe cuts a pattern through the applied colored dip surface to the base color below producing a checkered design. Alternating boxes in the pattern are ornamented with quatrefoils in a contrasting color. Another type of diceware design was produced by intersecting the checkered pattern with oak leaf or other borders. Still other diceware items mix the diceware pattern with bas-relief figures and other decorative applications. After its original production in the late eighteenth through the very early nineteenth century, diceware was revived in the last decades of the nineteenth century. It was revived once again in the late twentieth century for a number of limited edition projects.

Vase, four-color diceware (dip, pale blue ground, lilac and white with sage green quatrefoils on a polished basalt base), mark: not visible, ca. 1790. 8" h. *Courtesy of Leo Kaplan, Ltd. NYC.* $20,000-25,000.

Wine Cooler with Swan Handles, diceware (dip, dark blue with yellow quatrefoils), *"Roman Banquet,"* mark: Wedgwood (rare upper and lower case mark), ca. 1790. 12" x 7". *Courtesy of Leo Kaplan, Ltd. NYC.* $10,000-12,000.

Vase with Frog, diceware (dip, dark blue with sage green quatrefoils), mark: WEDGWOOD, ca. 1800, 6" h. *Courtesy of Skinner, Inc., Boston and Bolton, Ma.* $3000-5000.

Vase (388), diceware (dip, greenish yellow with blue quatrefoils), "Ulysses Staying the Chariot of Victory," mark: WEDGWOOD, ca. 1800, 7.5" x 4.5". *Courtesy of the Buten Collection of Wedgwood at the Sands Point Preserve, Sands Point, N.Y.* $2000-3000.

Chocolate Cup and Saucer, diceware (dip, black with yellow quatrefoils and lotus finial), mark: WEDGWOOD, ca. 1800, 4" x 5". *Courtesy of Dr. and Mrs. Victor Polikoff.* $2500-3500.

Teapot, diceware (dip, lilac with sage green quatrefoils), mark: WEDGWOOD, early 19th century, 4" h. *Courtesy of Skinner, Inc., Boston and Bolton, Ma.* $3000-4000.

Jug, diceware (dip, lilac with sage green quatrefoils), mark: WEDGWOOD, mid-19th century, 6" h. *Courtesy of Skinner, Inc., Boston and Bolton, Ma.* $1200-1500.

Vase (replaced cover), diceware (dip, black with yellow florets), *"Muses,"* mark: WEDGWOOD, 19th century, 7.375" h. *Courtesy of Skinner, Inc., Boston and Bolton, Ma.* $3500-4500.

Vase (missing cover), diceware (dip, black with yellow quatrefoils), *"Aurora" and "Psyche Bound to Tree by Cupids,"* mark: WEDGWOOD, ENGLAND, ca. 1900, 5.5" h. *Courtesy of Skinner, Inc., Boston and Bolton, Ma.* $1000-1200.

Tea Set, diceware (dip, black with yellow quatrefoils), marks: WEDGWOOD, 19th century, 3.875" h. (teapot), 4" h.(sugar), 3" h (creamer). *Courtesy of Skinner, Inc., Boston and Bolton, Ma.* $5000-7000.

Tobacco Jar, diceware (dip, sage green with lilac quatrefoils), mark: WEDGWOOD, MADE IN ENGLAND, 1972 (Limited Edition in the 'Wedgwood Masterpiece Collection'), 8" x 5". *Courtesy of the Kerner Collection.* $1000-1200.

Vase (Goblet), diceware (dip, pale blue with sage green quatrefoils, *"Queen Elizabeth II,"* mark: WEDGWOOD, MADE IN ENGLAND, 1976 (Limited Edition of 200 for Queen's Silver Jubilee), 5" x 3.25". *Courtesy of the Kerner Collection.* $500-700.

Vase (Goblet), diceware (dip, pale blue with sage green quatrefoils), *"George Washington,"* mark: WEDGWOOD, MADE IN ENGLAND, 1976, Printed in Gold "American Independence Bicentennial 1776-1976", 4.75" x 2.5". *Anonymous Private Collection.* $400-500.

Bowl, diceware (dip, pale blue with yellow quatrefoils), mark: WEDGWOOD, MADE IN ENGLAND, 1978 (Limited Edition), 3.5" x 8". *Courtesy of the Kerner Collection.* $800-1000.

Flower Pot with Frog, dip, diceware (dip, pale blue with yellow quatrefoils), mark: WEDGWOOD, MADE IN ENGLAND, ca. 1980, 5.5" x 4.25". *Courtesy of the Kerner Collection.* $800-1000.

Plate, strapware (dip, white with applied bright blue and yellow strapwork), mark: WEDGWOOD, ca. 1795, 8.5" diameter, *Courtesy of the Buten Collection of Wedgwood at the Sands Point Preserve, Sands Point, N.Y.* $3000-4000.

b. Strapware

Perhaps the rarest type of multicolored Wedgwood Jasper, strapware was produced only in the earliest years of Wedgwood and is an example of the art of ornamentation at its finest. Like diceware, strapware utilized a lathe to cut the pattern. However, the intricate strapware relief work was achieved entirely by painstaking hand application. The basket weaved pattern with horizontal and vertical strap work in different colors and designs is incredibly eye-catching. Often the use of a golden yellow color gives the item a very classical appearance. The amount of skill and time needed to produce work of this caliber must have made its cost too prohibitive for it to have been produced in large quantities or to be reintroduced at later dates.

Basket and Underplate, strapware , pale blue (dip) and green with white and buff strapwork), mark: WEDGWOOD, ca. 1795, 4" x 8.5". *Anonymous Private Collection.* $10,000-12,000.

Bough Pot, strapware (dip, bright blue bowl and white cover with applied white and yellow strapwork), mark: WEDGWOOD, ca. 1795, 4" x 8.75". *Courtesy of the Buten Collection of Wedgwood at the Sands Point Preserve, Sands Point, N.Y.* $3000-4000.

Flower Pot with Underplate, strapware (dip, white with lilac and sage green strapwork), mark: WEDGWOOD, ca. 1795, 4" x 4.5". *Courtesy of the Buten Collection of Wedgwood at the Sands Point Preserve, Sands Point, N.Y.* $3000-5000.

Tray, strapware (dip, white with applied bright blue and gold strapwork), mark: WEDGWOOD, ca. 1795, 10" x 8". *Courtesy of Drs. Elaine and Jeffrey Tulman.* $7500-9500.

Vase (missing lid), strapware (dip, white with applied bright blue and sage green strapwork), mark: WEDGWOOD, ca. 1800, 5" h. *Courtesy of Skinner, Inc., Boston and Bolton, Ma.* $2500-3500.

c. Sgraffito

A type of Jasper dip where a floral pattern is cut through to the white ground on various shaped jugs, boxes, tea sets, etc. The designs clearly show the influence of Japanese art. Though not a new technique, the examples shown in this book were basically the work of Harry Barnard (1862-1933) and were produced around the turn of the twentieth century. In contrast to the artists who were employed anonymously in the days of the first Josiah Wedgwood, Harry Barnard's signature is incised on all these pieces. In recent years some new types of prestige Jasper Sgraffito have been produced in very limited quantities.

Tea Set (St. Louis), dark blue (dip, sgraffito, signed by Harry Barnard), marks: WEDGWOOD, ENGLAND, 1896, 4.5" x 3.5" (teapot), 3.5" x 2" (creamer), 4" x 3" (sugar). *Courtesy of Adele Ierubino Barnett.* $1800-2000.

Mug (Upright), pale blue (dip, sgraffito, signed by Harry Barnard), mark: WEDGWOOD, ENGLAND, ca. 1895, 5.75" x 4.75". *Courtesy of the Buten Collection of Wedgwood at the Sands Point Preserve, Sands Point, N.Y.* $1200-1500.

Puff Box, lilac (dip, sgraffito, signed by Harry Barnard), mark: WEDGWOOD, ENGLAND, ca. 1900, 4" x 4.75". *Courtesy of Ellen Rubell.* $1500-1800.

Box (oblong), dark blue (dip, sgraffito, signed by Harry Barnard), mark: WEDGWOOD, ENGLAND, ca. 1895, 1.5" x 7". *Courtesy of the Buten Collection of Wedgwood at the Sands Point Preserve, Sands Point, N.Y.* $1000-1200.

Match Box, black (dip, sgraffito, signed by Harry Barnard), mark: WEDGWOOD, ENGLAND, ca. 1900, 3.875" l. *Courtesy of Skinner, Inc., Boston and Bolton, Ma.* $900-1100.

Bonbon Box (Bean), lilac (dip, sgraffito, signed by Harry Barnard), mark: WEDGWOOD, ENGLAND, ca. 1900, 2" x 3". *Courtesy of Ellen Rubell.* $1200-1500.

Teapot (146), black (dip, sgraffito, signed by Harry Barnard), mark: WEDGWOOD, ENGLAND, ca. 1900, 4" x 7". *Anonymous Private Collection.* $1800-2000.

Jug (Etruscan), black (dip, sgraffito, signed by Harry Barnard), mark: WEDGWOOD, ca. 1900, 6" h. *Courtesy of Skinner, Inc., Boston and Bolton, Ma.* $2000-3000.

Box (Pomade), dark blue (dip, sgraffito, signed by Harry Barnard), mark: WEDGWOOD, ENGLAND, ca. 1900, 2.75" diameter. *Courtesy of Skinner, Inc., Boston and Bolton, Ma.* $800-1000.

d. Sage Green and Lilac on White Jasper

The three previously shown categories of Wedgwood Jasper are all of the dip variety. Here we have examples of tricolor solid Jasper. The solid white ground is maintained and is ornamented with sage green and lilac relief. A number of different styles are employed with this color combination especially acanthus and bellflowers, or swags and cameos. Both useful ware like tea sets and decorative items like vases were made with this very attractive grouping of colors. Most examples of this type were produced from the last three decades of the nineteenth century through the early years of the twentieth.

Vase (missing lid), tricolor (solid, white with lilac and sage green relief), *"Classical Figure,"* mark: WEDGWOOD, ca. 1880, 8" x 6". *Courtesy of the Buten Collection of Wedgwood at the Sands Point Preserve, Sands Point, N.Y.* $800-1000.

Creamer, tricolor (solid, white with sage and lilac relief), mark: WEDGWOOD, ca. 1880, 2.5" x 2.5". *Anonymous Private Collection.* $800-1000.

Teapot, tricolor (solid, white with lilac and sage green relief), mark: WEDGWOOD, ca. 1870, 5.5" x 2.5". *Courtesy of the Donald and Marsha Levine Ceramics and Glass Collection at the Sands Point Preserve, Sands Point, N.Y.* $1000-1200.

Hair Receiver, tricolor (solid, white with sage green and lilac relief), mark: WEDGWOOD, late 19th century, 3.5" h. *Courtesy of Skinner, Inc., Boston and Bolton, Ma.* $1000-1200.

Covered Plate, tricolor (solid, white with lilac and sage green relief), mark: WEDGWOOD, ENGLAND, ca. 1900, 4" x 8.878". *Courtesy of Elizabeth and Paul Lauer.* $1200-1500.

Cup, tricolor (solid, white with lilac and sage green relief), mark: WEDGWOOD, ENGLAND, ca. 1900, 3.125" x 2.5". *Courtesy of Elizabeth and Paul Lauer.* $600-800.

Covered Jug or Chocolate Pot (Upright), tricolor (solid, white with sage green and lilac relief), mark: WEDGWOOD, ENGLAND, ca. 1900, 7.25 h. *Courtesy of Skinner, Inc., Boston and Bolton, Ma.* $1200-1500.

Tea Set, tricolor (solid, white with lilac and sage green relief), mark: WEDGWOOD, ENGLAND, ca. 1900, 6" x 6" (teapot), 4" x 4.5" (sugar), 4" x 4.75" (creamer). *Courtesy of Elizabeth and Paul Lauer.* $3000-4000.

Tea Set (146), tricolor (solid, white with sage green and lilac relief), mark: WEDGWOOD, ENGLAND, ca. 1900, 4.5" h (tea pot). . *Courtesy of Skinner, Inc., Boston and Bolton, Ma.* $2000-3000.

Flower Vase on Foot, tricolor (solid, white with sage green and lilac relief), mark: WEDGWOOD, ENGLAND, ca. 1900, 4.25" x 4.5". *Courtesy of Stamford Auction, Stamford, Ct.* $1000-1200.

e. Jasper Mounted on Decorative Metal

Shown here are some examples of Wedgwood Jasper that have been mounted on decorative metals such as brass, bronze, and ormolu, which is gilded brass or bronze. Not included here are the much more common useful pieces that have silver plated mounts, bases, covers, or handles (usually stamped EPNS for electroplated nickel silver). They will be found in the Gallery of Shapes especially among the biscuit barrels and dining miscellanea. Similarly, jewelry will be found in its own section. Some of the pieces shown in this section were created by mounting Wedgwood medallions on to metal items. Others are examples of mounting the metal to the pre-existing Wedgwood piece. In any case, the contrast between the brilliance of the shiny metal and the Wedgwood with its matte surface is very striking. Though most of the pieces shown predate the twentieth century, the mounting of Jasper continued well past that period.

Pair of Candelabra with prisms, mounted on brass, pale blue (solid), *"Boys at Play" and "French Revolution,"* mark: WEDGWOOD, ca. 1790, 11.5" x 4.5. *Courtesy of Edward L. Knowles.* $2500-3500.

Jewel Box, dark blue (dip) medallions mounted on brass, *"Sportive Love,"* mark: none visible, 19th century, 4.5" h. *Courtesy of Skinner, Inc., Boston and Bolton, Ma.* $1000-1200.

Bowl (Footed), dark blue (dip, with gilt metal mounts and handles), mark: WEDGWOOD, ca.1877, 7.5" h. *Courtesy of Skinner, Inc., Boston and Bolton, Ma.* $800-1000.

Ewer, diceware (dip, pale blue with sage green quatrefoils with silver plated copper base and handle), mark: not visible, c. 1870, 4.5" x 1.75". *Courtesy of the Buten Collection of Wedgwood at the Sands Point Preserve, Sands Point, N.Y.* $1000-1200.

Inkwell, brass body inset with pale blue Wedgwood medallions, marks not visible, ca. 1880, 5" x 7.75". *Courtesy of Julie and Lance Pearce.* $500-600.

Trophy Plate, pale blue (solid?, mounted on a brass footed bowl with 8 Jasper medallions), *"Bellerophon and Pegasus,"* etc., mark: not visible, ca. 1880, 12.75" X 3". *Courtesy of the Buten Collection of Wedgwood at the Sands Point Preserve, Sands Point, N.Y.* $900-1000.

Scale Set consisting of Five Medallions (pale blue) mounted on ormolu with a wooden base, mark: none visible, late 19th century, 8" w. *Courtesy of Skinner, Inc., Boston and Bolton, Ma.* $1500-1800.

Cistern, pale blue (dip, with brass base and mounts), *"Classical Figures,"* mark: WEDGWOOD, late 19th century, 6.375" h. *Courtesy of Skinner, Inc., Boston and Bolton, Ma.* $600-800.

Mantel Clock, pale blue plaques mounted on ormolu, *"Sacrifice Figures," etc.*, mark: none visible, late 19th century, 11" h. *Courtesy of Skinner, Inc., Boston and Bolton, Ma.* $1200-1500.

Pair of Candlesticks, pale blue (solid, mounted on ormolu), *"Hope and the Anchor," "Venus and Cupid,"etc.*, marks: none visible, late 19th century, 11" h. *Courtesy of Skinner, Inc., Boston and Bolton, Ma.* $1200-1500.

Pair of Vases, tricolor (dip, pale blue and lilac with ormolu mounts and handles), mark: WEDGWOOD, late 19th century, 10.625" h. . *Courtesy of Skinner, Inc., Boston and Bolton, Ma.* $4000-6000.

Door Knob, pale blue mounted on brass, *"Cupid as Oracle,"* mark: none visible, ca. 1890, 1.5" diameter (Wedgwood piece only). *Courtesy of Adele Ierubino Barnett.* $300-400.

Vase, lilac (dip) with bronze mountings, *"Calliope,"* mark: none visible, ca.1890, 5.25". *Anonymous Private Collection.* $700-800.

Eight Piece Desk Set (dark blue medallions mounted on sterling plated bronze), marks: WEDGWOOD, ca. 1920, various sizes, *Courtesy of Elizabeth and Paul Lauer.* $1500-2500.

f. Crimson Jasper

Except for their color, the Wedgwood Jasper shapes illustrated here are not very unusual or rare, yet crimson dip Jasper is one of the most sought after types of Wedgwood products. The entire line is basically an offshoot of Bas- Relief Ware that was produced early in the twentieth century for everyday use. There are no special or new shapes that are not also found in the more usual Wedgwood Jasper dip colors. Though probably utilized in trials in earlier periods the crimson color was introduced experimentally in 1910 for a brief time though the bulk of crimson Jasper that survives today was manufactured between 1929 and 1935.

As lovely as the new color was, it caused a lot of production headaches as the crimson color was unstable and tended to bleed into the white relief. As all imperfect pieces had to be discarded the manufacture of Jasper in crimson proved to be uneconomical and was thus discontinued. Naturally, this large amount of discarded rejects created a scarcity, as compared to other contemporary colors, and created the lively market that exists today among collectors. In the twenty-first century a similar color of solid Jasper called "wine" was introduced to entice this collectors' market. The pieces produced in wine in no way resemble their crimson predecessors yet they are sometimes offered on the internet as examples of crimson Jasper. *Caveat emptor!*

Butter Lugger, crimson (dip), *"Sacrifice Figures,"* mark: WEDGWOOD, ENGLAND, ca. 1925, 3.5" x 5.5". *Courtesy of David Kroun.* $1500-2000.

Chamber Candlestick (flat with snuffer), crimson (dip), mark: WEDGWOOD, ENGLAND, ca. 1910, "2.75" x 5.25". *Anonymous Private Collection.* $1000-1200.

Bonbon Box (Round), crimson (dip), *"Muses Watering Pegasus,"* mark: WEDGWOOD, ENGLAND, 1930, 4" x 5". *Anonymous Private Collection.* $1800-2000.

Tea Canister and Open Sugar or Slop Bowl, crimson (dip), *"Sacrifice to Peace" and "Aescalapius treating a Youth,"* marks: WEDGWOOD, ENGLAND, ca.1925, 5.75" x 3.25" (canister) and 2" x 3". *Anonymous Private Collection.* $1800-2000 and $800-1000.

Pair of Jugs (Dutch), crimson (dip), *"Sacrifice Figures," and "Ulysses Staying the Chariot of Victory,"* marks: WEDGWOOD, ENGLAND and WEDGWOOD, MADE IN ENGLAND, ca. 1925 - 1930, 5" x 6.25" and 2.5" x 3". *Anonymous Private Collection.* $1500-1800 and $800-1000.

Jug (Orange), crimson (dip), *"Euterpe,"* mark: WEDGWOOD, ENGLAND, ca. 1925, 6.5" x 8". *Anonymous Private Collection.* $1800-2000.

Mug (Upright) and Jug (Upright), crimson (dip), *"Sacrifice Figures,"* marks: WEDGWOOD, ENGLAND, ca. 1925, 5.25" x 4.25" (mug), 7.5" x 4.5" (jug), *Anonymous Private Collection.* $1500-1800 (each).

Five Ash or Pin Trays (Old Heart, Heart, Diamond, Spade and Club), crimson (dip), marks: WEDGWOOD, ENGLAND, ca. 1925, various sizes, *Anonymous Private Collection.* $800-1000 (each).

Five Boxes (Scalloped Bonbon, Bean Bonbon, Tooth Powder, Pomade and Match), crimson (dip), marks: WEDGWOOD, ENGLAND or WEDGWOOD, MADE IN ENGLAND, ca. 1920-1930, various sizes, *Anonymous Private Collection.* $1000-1200 (each).

Four Boxes (Square Bonbon, Heart Bonbon, Silver Bonbon and Laurel Pomade), crimson (dip), marks: WEDGWOOD, ENGLAND or WEDGWOOD, MADE IN ENGLAND, ca. 1920-1930, various sizes, *Anonymous Private Collection.* $1000-1200 (each).

Tea Set (146), crimson (dip), *"Sacrifice Figures," etc.*, mark: WEDGWOOD, ENGLAND, ca. 1920, 3.5" h. (teapot), 3.25" h. (sugar), 2" h. (creamer). *Courtesy of Skinner, Inc., Boston and Bolton, Ma.* $2500-3500.

Jug (Club), crimson (dip), *"Muses,"* mark: WEDGWOOD, ENGLAND, ca. 1920. *Courtesy of Skinner, Inc., Boston and Bolton, Ma.* $1800-2000.

g. Royalty

There has been a relationship between the Wedgwood Company and the British Crown practically from the beginning of the Company's existence. As a result of producing and supplying a new tea service for Queen Charlotte, Josiah Wedgwood was appointed as "Potter to Her Majesty" in 1766. This royal connection has been documented over the centuries on many types of Wedgwood products including Jasper. Coronations, royal weddings, royal trips and most prominent members of the royal family have been consistently commemorated. Shown in this section are Wedgwood Jasper items that depict every monarch who held the throne since the invention of Jasper as well as several other pieces with royal subjects. The monarchs are listed below with the years of their reigns:

George III (1760-1820)
George IV (1820-1830)
William IV (1830-1837)
Victoria (1837-1901)
Edward VII (1901-1910)
George V (1910-1936)
Edward VIII (1936)
George VI (1936-1952)
Elizabeth II (1952- to the present)

Pen Tray, light blue (dip), "Queen Victoria," mark: WEDGWOOD, ENGLAND, ca. 1895. 6" x 3.25". *Courtesy of Adele Ierubino Barnett.* $400-500.

Medallion, dark blue (dip) with polished lapidary edge, *"King George III,"* mark: WEDGWOOD, ca.1795, 1.75" diameter, *Courtesy of the Buten Collection of Wedgwood at the Sands Point Preserve, Sands Point, N.Y.* $1200-1500.

Plaque, pale blue (solid), *"King George IV,"* mark: WEDGWOOD, MADE IN ENGLAND, 1953, 6.25" x 5". *Courtesy of the Wedgwood Museum Trust, Barlaston, Staffordshire, England.* $150-250.

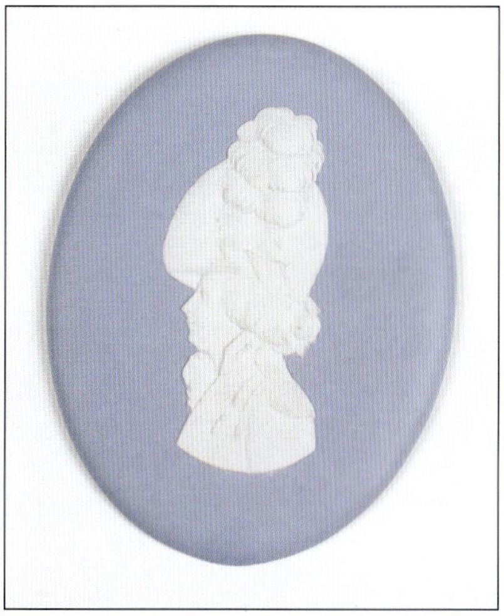

Plaque, yellow (dip), *"King Edward VII,"* marks: WEDGWOOD and KING EDWARD VII 1911, 5.25 x 5". *Courtesy of Dr. and Mrs. Victor Polikoff.* $650-850.

Plaque, pale blue (solid), *"King William IV,"* mark: WEDGWOOD, MADE IN ENGLAND, 1970, 4.25" x 3.25". *Courtesy of the Wedgwood Museum Trust, Barlaston, Staffordshire, England.* $150-250.

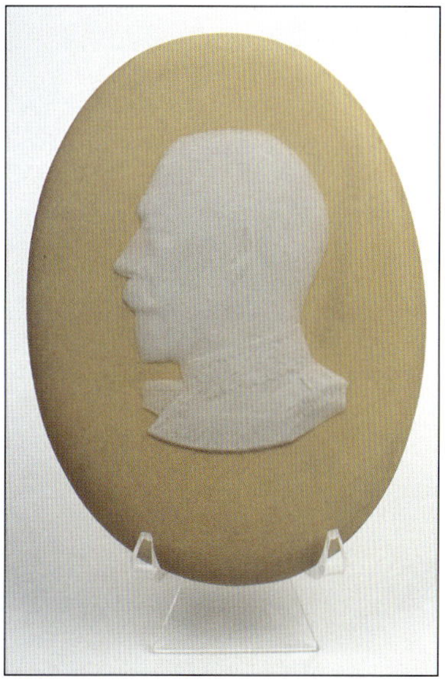

Plaque, yellow (dip), *"King George V,"* mark: WEDGWOOD, 1911, 4.5" x 3". *Courtesy of the Buten Collection of Wedgwood at the Sands Point Preserve, Sands Point, N.Y.* $1000-1200.

Teapot (146), dark blue (dip), *"King Edward VIII,"* mark: WEDGWOOD, MADE IN ENGLAND. Produced in 1937 for Edward's coronation. 6" x 4.5. *Courtesy of Adele Ierubino Barnett.* $300-400.

Mug (Upright), dark blue (dip), *"King George VI,"* mark: WEDGWOOD, MADE IN ENGLAND, 1939 (Issued to commemorate King's visit to Canada), 4.5" x 5." *Courtesy of Dr. and Mrs. Victor Polikoff.* $350-450.

Bonbon Box (Heart). Royal Blue (solid), *"Queen Elizabeth II,"* mark: WEDGWOOD, MADE IN ENGLAND. Produced in 1977 for the Queen's Silver Jubilee, 5" x 3.5". *Courtesy of Adele Ierubino Barnett.* $100-200.

Tea Canister, tricolor (solid, sage green and lilac), *"Prince Charles,"* limited edition produced for Royal Wedding of Prince Charles and Princess Diana in July 1981, mark: WEDGWOOD, MADE IN ENGLAND, 6.5" x 4". *Courtesy of David Kroun.* $800-1000.

Vase (1200), pale sage green, *"Queen Charlotte,"* mark: WEDGWOOD, ca. 1790. 14" x 5.5". *Anonymous Private Collection.* $2000-2500.

Plate, five-color (solid, pale blue, yellow, lilac and sage green), *"Queen Elizabeth II,"* mark: WEDGWOOD, MADE IN ENGLAND, 1977 (Limited Edition of 750 for Queen's Silver Jubilee), 8.875" diameter. *Courtesy of Skinner, Inc., Boston and Bolton, Ma.* $500-700.

h. Commemoratives and Souvenirs

In addition to the British monarchs, many other illustrious persons and themes have been commemorated on Wedgwood Jasper. In the early years contemporary events such as the French Revolution and developments in Germany and Austria were shown on medallions. American subjects have always been prominent, such as the American Centennial (1876) and Bicentennial (1976), presidents, and the space program. Josiah Wedgwood and his Company's history and achievements have also been frequently memorialized in Jasper as have historical events in Australia and other parts of the British Commonwealth. Also shown in this section are souvenir pieces known as Arms Ware which depict the crests or shields of cities and towns in the United Kingdom as well as overseas outposts of the then British Empire. Other types of souvenir items were those issued for a particular company or special event. All of these kinds of issues have been highly collectible to a much wider audience than just the Wedgwood specialist.

Medallion, dark blue (dip, with lapidary polished edge), *"Germany in the character of Minerva encouraging Art and Labour with Peace to work for the prosperity of the Empire,"* (one of the "German Cameos"), mark: WEDGWOOD, ca. 1790, 2" diameter. *Courtesy of Drs. Elaine and Jeffrey Tulman*. $900-1000.

Toothpick Holder, dark blue (dip), *"Josiah Wedgwood,"* mark: WEDGWOOD, ENGLAND, 1906 (Produced for opening of the Wedgwood Museum), 1.5" x 2". *Author's Collection*. $150-250.

Loving Mug or Tyg , dark blue (dip), *"Wembley British Empire Exhibition Arms,"* mark: WEDGWOOD, MADE IN ENGLAND, 1924, 2" x 2.25". *Anonymous Private Collection*. $200-300.

Match Box (Square), black (dip), *"Wembley British Empire Exhibition Arms,"* mark: WEDGWOOD, MADE IN ENGLAND, 1924, 3.5" x 1.5". *Courtesy of the Buten Collection of Wedgwood at the Sands Point Preserve, Sands Point, N.Y.* $400-500.

Tea Set (Brewster), olive green (dip), *"George Washington"* and *"Benjamin Franklin,"* mark: WEDGWOOD, ENGLAND, ca. 1925, 3.75" x 7.25" (teapot). *Courtesy of the Kerner Collection.* $800-1000.

Jug (Orange), olive green (dip), *"Benjamin Franklin,"* mark: WEDGWOOD, ENGLAND, ca. 1930, 6" x 7.25". *Courtesy of the Kerner Collection.* $400-600.

Tea Set (146), dark blue (dip), *"The Half Moon,"* mark: WEDGWOOD, MADE IN ENGLAND, 1939 (Made for B Altman & Co., New York to commemorate the sesquicentennial of George Washington's Inauguration in 1789), 5" x 9" (teapot), 4" x 5" (sugar bowl), 2.5" x 5" (creamer), *Courtesy of Marcy Nirschel.* $800-1000 (for set).

Posy Pot, dark blue (dip), *"American Eagle,"* mark: WEDGWOOD, MADE IN ENGLAND, 1939 (Made for B Altman & Co., New York to commemorate the sesquicentennial of George Washington's Inauguration in 1789), 5" x 4". *Courtesy of Marcy Nirschel.* $250-350.

Stamp that appears on bottoms of previous three items.

Closeup of "The Half Moon" in previous items.

Bonbon Box (Square), dark blue (dip), *"The Half Moon,"* mark: WEDGWOOD, MADE IN ENGLAND, 1939 (Made for B Altman & Co., New York to commemorate the sesquicentennial of George Washington's Inauguration in 1789), 4" x 4". *Courtesy of Marcy Nirschel.* $250-350.

Pin Tray, pale blue (solid), *"Captain James Cook,"* mark: WEDGWOOD, MADE IN ENGLAND, 1970 (Issued to commemorate the Bicentennial of Captain Cook's "discovery" of Australia), 4.675" diameter. *Author's Collection.* $75-125.

Vase, tricolor (solid pale and Portland blue with engine turning), mark: WEDGWOOD, MADE IN ENGLAND®, 1975, (limited edition of 200 stamped in gold "The Company of Cutlers in Hallamshire"), 7" x 4.5". *Courtesy of Adele Ierubino Barnett.* $500-600.

Vase (Goblet), diceware (dip, pale blue with sage green quatrefoils), *"George Washington and Thomas Jefferson,"* mark: WEDGWOOD, MADE IN ENGLAND, 1976, Printed in Gold "American Independence Bicentennial 1776-1976", 4.75" x 2.5". *Anonymous Private Collection.* $400-500.

Trophy Plate. tricolor (dip, black with lilac, sage green and white relief, "Josiah Wedgwood," limited edition produced for 250th anniversary of Josiah Wedgwood'd birth, mark: WEDGWOOD, MADE IN ENGLAND, 1980, 8.5" diameter. *Courtesy of David Kroun.* $700-800.

Self Framed Plaque, pale blue (solid, with black on terracotta frame), *"Josiah WEDGWOOD,"* Limited Edition of 250 for 250th anniversary of Josiah-Wedgwood's birth, mark: WEDGWOOD, MADE IN ENGLAND, 1980. 5" x 4.5". *Courtesy of David Kroun.* $500-600.

Other side of previous. "Josiah Wedgwood."

Close-up of above item showing rams' heads and stamp.

Vase (1200 with pierced lid), pale blue (solid), "Sarah Wedgwood," mark: WEDGWOOD, MADE IN ENGLAND, 1984 (limited edition of 225 to mark the 225th anniversary of the Wedgwood Company). 11.25" x 5.25". *Courtesy of Adele Ierubino Barnett.* $1000-1200.

Two Vases (Miniatures – Arms Ware), dark blue and pale blue (dip), *"Arms of Bournemouth and Stratford-upon-Avon,"* marks: WEDGWOOD, ENGLAND, ca. 1900, 2.5" h. *Courtesy of Adele Ierubino Barnett.* $100-200 (each)

Teapot (Miniature – Arms Ware), dark blue (dip), *"Arms of Torquay,"* mark: WEDGWOOD, ca. 1900, 2.3" x 3". *Author's Collection.* $300-400.

Vase (Miniature – Arms Ware), dark blue (dip), *"Arms of Rickmansworth,"* mark: WEDGWOOD, ENGLAND, ca. 1900, 3" x 1.5". *Author's Collection.* $200-300.

Jug (Upright), dark blue (dip), *"Arms of Bermuda,"* mark: WEDGWOOD, ca. 1900, 3.5" x 2.75". *Courtesy of Marcy Nirschel.* $150-250.

II. *The Gallery of Shapes and Other Jasper Items*

The majority of the Wedgwood Jasper in this book will be shown in the pages ahead. I have divided this section into specific as well as broad categories with some categories much broader than others. Within most categories a chronological approach is utilized to show both the continuity and change in the Wedgwood items depicted. Some categories are subdivided to emphasize special types, and the largest section, vases, is broken up into several divisions to manage different types of classifications. Other examples of objects in most of these categories can be found in my previous book *Wedgwood Jasper Ware, A Shape Book and Collector's Guide.*

a. Biscuit Barrels

Biscuit Barrels, also known as biscuit jars or cookie jars, are among the most commonly found types of older Wedgwood Jasper, making it obvious that they were produced in prodigious quantities and found their way into numerous homes. Most of them have silver-plated (E.P.N.S.) mounts, lids and handles but there are also some models that are purely ceramic. Several examples shown here were custom produced for specific companies.

Biscuit Barrel, lilac (dip, with silver plated mount, lid and handle), *"Panathenea Festival Cavalrymen,"* mark: WEDGWOOD, ca. 1869, 7.5" h. *Courtesy of Skinner, Inc., Boston and Bolton, Ma.* $700-900.

Biscuit Barrel, tricolor (dip, dark blue with yellow lattice work ornamentation and silver plate mount, lid and handle), mark: WEDGWOOD, ca. 1882, 5.125" h. *Courtesy of Skinner, Inc., Boston and Bolton, Ma.* $900-1100.

Biscuit Barrel, tricolor (dip, sage green and lilac with silver plated mount, cover and handle), *"Dipping of Achilles," etc.*, mark: WEDGWOOD, late 19th century, 5.5" h. *Courtesy of Skinner, Inc., Boston and Bolton, Ma.* $800-1000.

Biscuit Barrel, diceware (dip, sage green with yellow quatrefoils and silver plated mount, lid and handle), *"Cupids at Play,"* mark: WEDGWOOD, late 19th century, 7.675" h. *Courtesy of Skinner, Inc., Boston and Bolton, Ma.* $1800-2000.

Biscuit Jar, sage green (dip), *"Dancing Hours,"* mark: WEDGWOOD, MCVITTIE & PRICE, 1906, 7.5" X 6.5". *Courtesy of the Kerner Collection.* $700-900.

Biscuit Jar (Upright), dark blue (dip), *"Marquis de Lafayette,"* mark: WEDGWOOD, ENGLAND, ca. 1900, 6.5" x 4.5". *Courtesy of the Kerner Collection.* $500-600.

Biscuit Barrel, tricolor (dip, pale blue and sage green with silver plated mount, lid and handle), *"Panathenea Festival Cavalryman,"* mark: WEDGWOOD, late 19th century, 6.125" h. *Courtesy of Skinner, Inc., Boston and Bolton, Ma.* $1200-1500.

Biscuit Jar, black (dip). *"Egyptian Motifs,"* mark: WEDGWOOD, ca. 1911 (produced for W.T. Lamb & Sons), 6.5". *Courtesy of Skinner, Inc., Boston and Bolton, Ma.* $1200-1500.

Biscuit Barrel (1674), dark blue (dip, with silver plated mount, cover and handle), *"Caperns Birds,"* mark WEDGWOOD, MADE IN ENGLAND and CAPERNS, LTD., BRISTOL, 1934, 5" x 5.5". *Courtesy of the Kerner Collection.* $500-700.

Biscuit Jar (Upright), black (dip). *"Egyptian Motifs,"* mark: WEDGWOOD, ca. 1911 (produced for W.T. Lamb & Sons), 5.25". *Courtesy of Skinner, Inc., Boston and Bolton, Ma.* $1000-1200.

b. Bowls

Wedgwood has produced bowls in Jasper since the eighteenth century. They range from the ordinary to the elaborate and, in size, from tiny to quite large. Many can be found with mounts, especially if they are slated for use in the kitchen.

Dancing Hours Bowls

These elegant bowls are wonderful examples of classic Wedgwood design, as hardly any other relief figures are so easily recognizable. First used in the eighteenth century and generally attributed to John Flaxman Jr, (1755-1826) these figures still grace Wedgwood products today. Dancing Hours bowls have always been offered as prestige pieces, made totally of Jasper while most other contemporary Jasper production was made in part from a lesser stoneware formulation.

Dancing Hours Bowl, black (solid), mark: WEDGWOOD, ca. 1880, 3" x 4.5". *Courtesy of the Kerner Collection.* $700-900.

Dancing Hours Bowl, dark blue (dip), mark: WEDGWOOD, ca. 1880, 5.25" x 12.5".*Courtesy of the Kerner Collection.* $2500-3000.

Dancing Hours Bowl, sage green (dip), mark: WEDGWOOD, ca. 1890, 4" x 10". *Courtesy of the Kerner Collection.* $1500-1800.

Dancing Hours Bowl, yellow buff and black (dip), mark: WEDGWOOD, ETRURIA ENGLAND, ca. 1895, 10.25" x 5". *Courtesy of the Donald and Marsha Levine Ceramics and Glass Collection at the Sands Point Preserve, Sands Point, N.Y.* $2000-3000.

Dancing Hours Bowl, tricolor (dip, lilac and sage green), mark: WEDGWOOD, MADE IN ENGLAND, 1959, 4.5" x 10". *Anonymous Private Collection.* $4000-6000.

Dancing Hours Bowl, terracotta (solid, with black relief), mark: WEDGWOOD, MADE IN ENGLAND, 1959, 4" x 10". *Courtesy of the Kerner Collection.* $500-700.

Dancing Hours Bowl, black (solid, with terracotta relief), mark: WEDGWOOD, MADE IN ENGLAND, 1980, 4" x 10". *Courtesy of the Kerner Collection.* $500-700.

Dancing Hours Bowl, gray (solid), mark: WEDGWOOD, MADE IN ENGLAND, 1994, 4" x 10". *Courtesy of the Kerner Collection.* $600-800.

Dancing Hours Bowl, Portland blue (solid, with white and light blue marbling), mark: WEDGWOOD, MADE IN ENGLAND, 2003 (custom made for owner), 4" x 8". *Courtesy of the Kerner Collection.* $1000-1200.

Other Bowls

Here is a wide gamut of bowl types from delicate examples of early Wedgwood workmanship to the more workaday products of later centuries. Salad bowls are frequently found with a matching set of serving pieces. Notice the large variety of shapes that are represented among this rather small selection as well as the example of one shape ornamented with three entirely different designs.

Bowl (footed), pale blue (solid), *"Boys at Play,"* mark: WEDGWOOD, ca. 1790, 9" x 5.5". *Courtesy of the Buten Collection of Wedgwood at the Sands Point Preserve, Sands Point, N.Y.* $1500-2000.

Bowl, slate blue (dip, with engine turning), *"Boys at Play," etc.*, mark: WEDGWOOD, ca. 1790, 3.25" X 7". *Courtesy of Drs. Elaine and Jeffrey Tulman..* $3000-4000.

Bowl, sage green and white (dip, with engine turning), mark: WEDGWOOD, ca. 1790, 1.75" x 3.25. *Courtesy of Drs. Elaine and Jeffrey Tulman.* $2000-3000.

Bowl, pale blue (solid, with lapidary polished interior), *"Domestic Employment,"* mark: WEDGWOOD, ca. 1790, 3.5" x 8.5". *Courtesy of Drs. Elaine and Jeffrey Tulman.* $3500-4000.

Bowl, lilac (dip, with engine turning), *"Boys at Play,"* mark: WEDGWOOD, ca. 1795, 2.25" x 5". *Courtesy of Ellen Rubell.* $1200-1500.

Three Bowls (Flanged), dark blue (dip), bottom to top: *"Foliage and Star Pattern," "Sacrifice Figures," "Aesculapius Treating a Youth,"* marks: WEDGWOOD, ca. 1820, 1890, 1870, 3.75" x 7", 3" x 6", 3" x 5.5". *Author's Collection.* $600-700, $300-400, $400-500.

Covered Bowl and Stand (probably not originally matched), pale blue (solid), mark: WEDGWOOD, 18th century, 5.25" w. *Courtesy of Skinner, Inc., Boston and Bolton, Ma.* $1000-1200.

Bowl, sage green (dip), *"Bacchanalian Figure,"* mark: WEDGWOOD, ca. 1820, 3.5" x 8.25". *Courtesy of the Buten Collection of Wedgwood at the Sands Point Preserve, Sands Point, N.Y.* $1000-1200.

Bowl (Montieth), dark blue (dip, with silver plated mount), *"Dipping of Achilles," etc.*, mark: WEDGWOOD, ca. 1880, 4" x 9". *Anonymous Private Collection.* $800-1000.

Bowl (Flanged), dark blue (dip), *"Aesculapius Treating a Youth" and "Zephyrs,"* mark: WEDGWOOD, ca. 1880, 3" x 5.5". *Author's Collection.* $400-500.

Bowl (Footed), dark blue (dip, with silver plated mount), mark: WEDGWOOD, ca. 1890, 3..25" x 4.25". *Anonymous Private Collection.* $300-400.

Salad Bowl (#3), tricolor (dip, dark blue and pale blue with silver plated mount), *"Sacrifice Figures,"* mark: WEDGWOOD, ca. 1890, 4" x 9". *Courtesy of the Kerner Collection.* $700-900.

Salad Bowl, yellow buff (dip, with black relief), mark: WEDGWOOD, ca. 1930, 4.5" x 9". *Courtesy of the Kerner Collection.* $800-1000.

Salad Bowl, tricolor (dip, sage green and lilac with silver plated mount), *"Three Graces," etc.*, mark: WEDGWOOD, ca. 1890, 4.75" x 8". *Courtesy of the Kerner Collection.* $1000-1200.

Pair of Footed Bowls, yellow buff (dip, with black relief), *"Cupids,"* mark: WEDGWOOD, ca. 1930, 5.75" h. *Courtesy of Skinner, Inc., Boston and Bolton, Ma.* $1000-1200.

Bowl (fluted, designed by Norman Wilson), very pale blue (solid), mark: WEDGWOOD, MADE IN ENGLAND, 1954, 10.5" x 4.25. *Courtesy of Adele Ierubino Barnett.* $600-700.

Bowl (Acanthus), tricolor (dip, lilac and sage green), mark: WEDGWOOD, MADE IN ENGLAND, 1959, 4.5" x 10". *Anonymous Private Collection.* $3500-4000.

Bowl (Egyptian Motifs), black (solid, with terracotta relief), mark: WEDGWOOD, MADE IN ENGLAND, 1978, 8" x 3.5". *Courtesy of David Kroun.* $800-900.

Bowl (Sacrifice), gray (solid), *"Sacrifice Figures,"* mark: WEDGWOOD, MADE IN ENGLAND, 1990, 4" x 8". *Courtesy of the Kerner Collection.* $300-400.

Bowl (Arabesque Footed). taupe (solid), mark: WEDGWOOD, MADE IN ENGLAND, 2004 (limited edition of 250 signed by Lord Wedgwood), 8" x 3.5". *Courtesy of David Kroun.* $900-1000.

c. Boxes

Definitely among the most useful items in the Wedgwood Jasper catalog, boxes come in a vast variety of shapes and sizes and serve a wide variety of functions. They have been made since the eighteenth century and are still popular today. Only a small group is shown here as other types have been assigned to different categories. Most boxes consist of a base and a lid, while some are either a single piece or have been put together by mounting a Wedgwood medallion on a box of another material.

Patch Box, sage green medallion on ivory box, *"Classical Figures,"* mark: none, visible, ca. 1800, 0.75" x 3.5". *Courtesy of Dr. and Mrs. Victor Polikoff.* $800-1000.

Paint Chest, pale blue (solid), "Boys at Play," mark: WEDGWOOD, 1790, 6.5" x 2". *Anonymous Private Collection.* $2000-2500.

Pomade Box (Upright), dark blue (dip), *"Charlotte at the Tomb of Werther" and "Cupid as Oracle,"* mark: WEDGWOOD, ca. 1890, 2.25" x 3". *Author's Collection.* $200-300.

Patch Box, lilac (dip) mounted on ivory, *"Sportive Love" and "Sacrifice Figures,"* mark: WEDGWOOD, ca. 1800, .75" x 3.25". *Courtesy of the Buten Collection of Wedgwood at the Sands Point Preserve, Sands Point, N.Y.* $1200-1500.

Bonbon Box (Round), white (solid, with sage green relief), *"Venus Hiding Cupid's Arrows,"* mark: WEDGWOOD, ENGLAND, ca. 1900, 4" x 5". *Anonymous Private Collection.* $600-800.

Fan Box, dark blue (dip), *"Ulysses Staying the Chariot of Victory,"* mark: WEDGWOOD, ENGLAND, ca. 1900, 1.5" x 5". *Author's Collection.* $400-500.

Rectangular Box, dark blue (dip), mark: WEDGWOOD, MADE IN ENGLAND, ca.1920, 5" x 3.5 x 1.5. *Courtesy of Adele Ierubino Barnett.* $150-250.

Pomade Box (Laurel), lilac (dip), *"Sacrifice to Peace,"* mark: WEDGWOOD, ENGLAND, ca. 1900, 3.5" x 2.5". *Courtesy of Ellen Rubell.* $500-600.

Powder Box (Upright), crimson (dip), *"Group With Cage,"* mark: WEDGWOOD, ENGLAND, ca. 1925, 3.25" X 5.25". *Courtesy of Jeffrey S. Milkins.* $1800-2000.

Box, tricolor (solid, pale and Portland blue), *"Apollo,"* mark: WEDGWOOD®, BICENTENARY, 1795-1995,MADE IN ENGLAND (for the bicentenary of the death of Josiah Wedgwood), 1" x 3". *Author's Collection.* $50-75.

d. Candleholders

Electric lighting has only illuminated a small fraction of human history. Prior to the Age of Edison candles were king. The elegant home needed attractive holders for the omnipresent candles and Wedgwood always endeavored to fill that need. There have been many varieties of Jasper candleholders over the last two-and-a-half centuries and they have ranged from the elaborately ornate to the most spartanly unadorned. Most have been freestanding while others could be hand held or hung on walls.

Letter Box, olive green (dip), *"Sacrifice Figures,"* mark: WEDGWOOD, ENGLAND, ca. 1930, 6" x 5". *Anonymous Private Collection.* $600-800.

Triton Candlestick, pale blue and white (solid), mark: WEDGWOOD, ca. 1790, 11" x 4". *Anonymous Private Collection.* $6000-7000.

Pair of Candlesticks, pale blue and white (solid), *"Ceres and Cybele,"* mark: WEDGWOOD, ca. 1790, 12.5" x 5". *Courtesy of Jeffrey S. Milkins.* $4000-6000.

Pair of Sphinx Candlesticks, bright blue (dip), mark: WEDG-WOOD, ca. 1795, 5.625" x 6.5. ". *Courtesy of the Donald and Marsha Levine Ceramics and Glass Collection at the Sands Point Preserve, Sands Point, N.Y.* $4000-6000.

Pair of Tree Form Candlesticks, pale blue and white (solid),*"Cupids as Autumn and Winter,"* mark: WEDGWOOD, ca. 1795, 10.75" x 4.5". *Courtesy of the Donald and Marsha Levine Ceramics and Glass Collection at the Sands Point Preserve, Sands Point, N.Y.* $5000-6000.

Candle Holder (Lustre), tricolor (dip, dark blue and sage green with brass mounts and prisms), *"Cupid as Oracle,"* mark: WEDGWOOD, ca. 1800, 9.75" x 4.75. *Courtesy of Edward L. Knowles.* $1800-2000.

Candlesticks, pale blue (dip, with white figures), *"Pomona,"* mark: WEDGWOOD, ca. 1800, 10.5" h. *Courtesy of Skinner, Inc., Boston and Bolton, Ma.* $1200-1500.

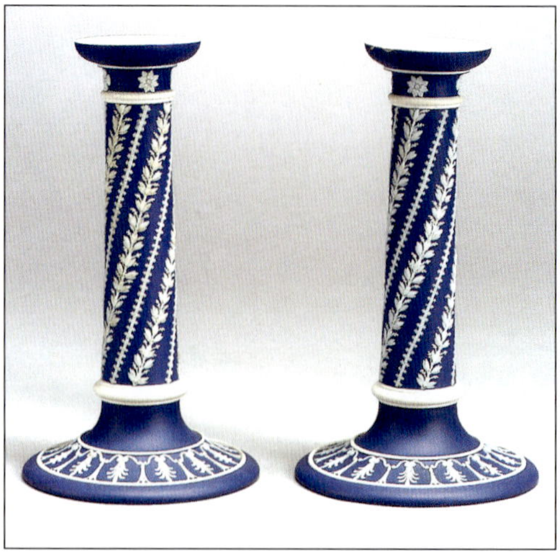

Candle Holder (Lustre) dark blue (dip, with prisms), *"Apollo,"* mark: WEDGWOOD, ca. 1800, 14.5" x 5". *Courtesy of Elizabeth and Paul Lauer.* $1500-1800.

Pair of Candlesticks, dark blue (dip), mark: WEDGWOOD, early 19th century, 8" h. *Courtesy of Skinner, Inc., Boston and Bolton, Ma.* $800-1000.

Pair of Candlesticks, lilac and white (dip), *"Ceres,"* mark: WEDGWOOD, TLW = 1868, 9.25" x.4.25". *Courtesy of Jeffrey S. Milkins.* $3500-4000.

Pair of Octagon Foot Candlesticks, dark blue (dip, with no ornamentation), mark: WEDGWOOD, ca. 1880, 7" x 4.5". *Courtesy of Adele Ierubino Barnett.* $500-600.

Pair of Candle Sconces, sage green (dip), *"Aurora,"* mark: WEDGWOOD, ca. 1880, size unknown, *Courtesy of Shapiro Auctions, Australia.* $1200-1500.

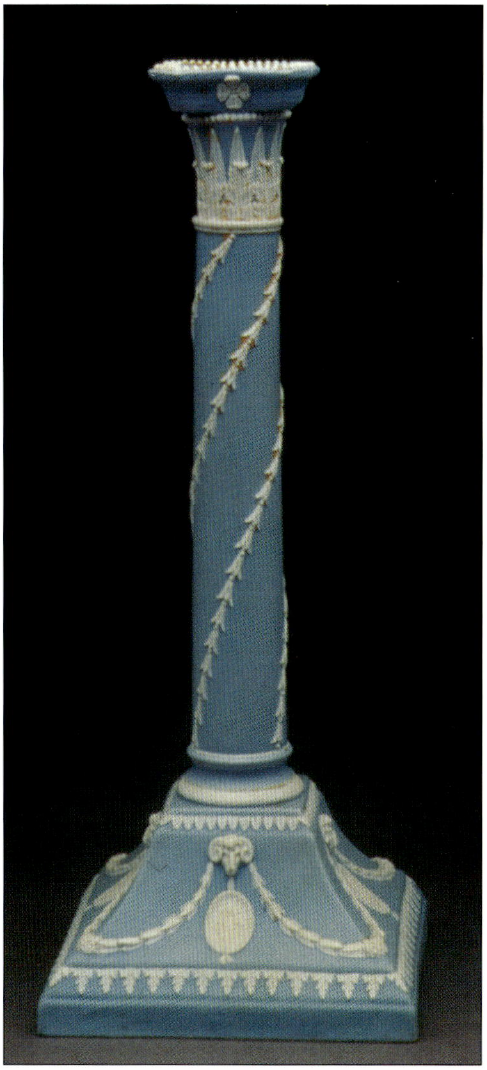

Candlestick, pale blue (dip), mark: WEDGWOOD, late 19th century, 11.75" h. *Courtesy of Skinner, Inc., Boston and Bolton, Ma.* $600-800.

Pair of Candlesticks, tricolor (solid, white with sage green and lilac relief), mark: WEDGWOOD, late 19th century, 11.25" h. *Courtesy of Skinner, Inc., Boston and Bolton, Ma.* $1500-1800.

Pair of Candlesticks (Acanthus), yellow buff (dip, with black relief), mark: WEDGWOOD, ENGLAND, ca. 1930, 8" h. *Courtesy of Skinner, Inc., Boston and Bolton, Ma.* $900-1100.

Pair of Candlesticks, yellow buff (dip, with black relief), mark: WEDGWOOD, ENGLAND, ca. 1930, 4.25" h. *Courtesy of Skinner, Inc., Boston and Bolton, Ma.* $1200-1500.

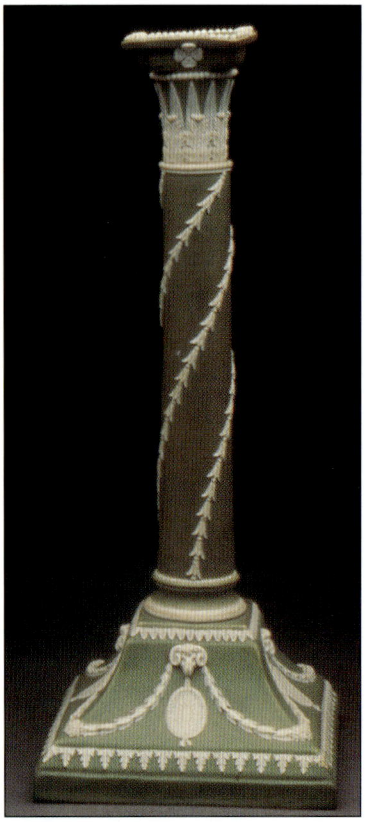

Candlestick, sage green (dip), mark: WEDGWOOD, late 19th century, 11.5" h. *Courtesy of Skinner, Inc., Boston and Bolton, Ma.* $600-800.

Pair of Candlesticks, primrose (solid) with terra cotta relief, mark: WEDGWOOD, MADE IN ENGLAND, ca. 1980, 5.25" x 2.5". *Courtesy of the Buten Collection of Wedgwood at the Sands Point Preserve, Sands Point, N.Y.* $500-600.

Pair of Contour Interiors Candlesticks, Portland Blue with silver etching (solid). Mark: WEDGWOOD, MADE IN ENGLAND + INTERIORS, 1999, 6.25" x 3.25". *Courtesy of Adele Ierubino Barnett.* $100-200.

Chess Men (designed by Arnold Machin), pale blue and white (solid), mark: WEDGWOOD, MADE IN ENGLAND, ca. 1940, 5.625" h. (king), *Courtesy of Bob and Lucie Reichner.* $3000-4000.

e. Chess Men

The ancient game of chess has always inspired artists to create beautiful pieces to enhance the pleasure of the playing. In Josiah Wedgwood's constant striving to raise the work of the potter to the level of the artist, the creation of a set of chessmen shows how successful he was. John Flaxman designed the first Wedgwood Jasper chess set in 1783-4 and over a hundred sets were sold over the next three decades. The queen is supposedly modeled after the famous actress Sarah Siddons. This set has been reproduced several times up to the present day. Arnold Machin (1911-1999), whose portraits of Queen Elizabeth II are widely seen on British stamps and coins, created a new set in 1940 in a somewhat more abstract design. In our own twenty-first century, an even newer design is being produced in several colors for special orders. All of these sets are highly prized acquisitions and even individual chess pieces can command very high prices.

Close-up of item below showing a King and Queen.

Chess Men (complete including Jesters as well as Bishops designed by John Flaxman Jr.), lilac and white and pale blue and white (dip), mark: WEDGWOOD, ca. 1785. *Courtesy of Jeffrey S. Milkins.* $50,00-60,000

Another view of above item

f. Clock Cases and Faces

Wedgwood has been producing clock cases for general production in Jasper since the late nineteenth century. As can be seen here, they were made in a variety of shapes and colors. The most usual types found are built around an upright rectangular base that has been elaborated in various ways. Earlier models had clock mechanisms built by various manufacturers while recent versions are powered by batteries and have the Wedgwood name on the dial. Also shown here is an example of a beautifully ornate clock face from the nineteenth century.

Another view of above item

Chess Men, marbled blue and white (solid), mark: WEDGWOOD, ENGLAND, 2004, 3.5" h. (king), *Courtesy of Bob and Lucie Reichner*. ca. $2000-2500.

Clock Case (Tempus Fugit), tricolor (solid, white with sage green and lilac relief), *"Father Time" and "Domestic Employment,"* mark: WEDGWOOD, late 19th century, 8" h. *Courtesy of Skinner, Inc., Boston and Bolton, Ma.* $1200-1500.

Clock Face, tricolor (solid, pale and dark blue), mark: WEDG-WOOD, late 19th century, 11.625" h. *Courtesy of Skinner, Inc., Boston and Bolton, Ma.* $1500-1800.

Clock Case, pale blue (dip), *"Sacrifice Figures,* and *"Boys at Play,"* mark: WEDGWOOD, ca. 1890, 7" x 5". *Anonymous Private Collection.* $1200-1500.

Clock Case, dark blue (dip), *"Zephyr,"* mark: WEDGWOOD, late 19th century, 5.25" h. *Courtesy of Skinner, Inc., Boston and Bolton, Ma.* $700-900.

Clock Case, sage green (dip), mark: WEDGWOOD, ENGLAND, ca. 1900, 8" x 4.5". *Anonymous Private Collection.* $1000-1200.

Clock Case (Tall A), dark blue (dip), *"Cupids at Play,"* mark: WEDGWOOD, ENGLAND, ca. 1900, 6.5" x 3.5". *Author's Collection.* $1000-1200.

Clock Case, pale blue (dip), *"Sacrifice Figures,"* mark: WEDGWOOD, ENGLAND, ca. 1900, 13.325" h. *Courtesy of Skinner, Inc., Boston and Bolton, Ma.* $1000-1200.

Clock Case, pale blue (dip), *"Cupid on Pedestal,"* mark: WEDGWOOD, ENGLAND, ca. 1900, 12.675" h. *Courtesy of Skinner, Inc., Boston and Bolton, Ma.* $1000-1200.

Clock Case (Vase Top), dark blue (dip), *"Offering to Peace,"* mark: WEDGWOOD, ENGLAND, ca. 1900, 8.5" h. *Courtesy of Skinner, Inc., Boston and Bolton, Ma.* $800-1000.

Garniture (Clock Case, Pairs of Vases and Candlesticks), yellow buff (dip, with black relief), *"Dipping of Achilles," etc.*, marks: WEDGWOOD, ETRURIA, ENGLAND, ca. 1930, 13" h. (clock), 12" h. (vases), 9" h. (candlesticks). *Courtesy of Skinner, Inc., Boston and Bolton, Ma.* $4000-6000.

Clock Case, yellow (solid, with black relief), mark: WEDGWOOD, MADE IN ENGLAND, ca. 2000, 4.25" x 3". *Courtesy of David Kroun.* $200-300.

g. Cups and Saucers

There have been countless examples of Wedgwood Jasper cups and saucers since the earliest years of the Company. They can be small works of art meant only for display or objects produced for everyday use. The cylindrical cups are usually designated as cans and are meant for coffee. Shown here are mostly the more ornate varieties that were produced between the eighteenth and the early twentieth centuries. Reproductions of some of these classic models have been issued in recent years, though most Jasper cups and saucers produced since World War II do not even attempt to look much more than functional.

Tea Bowl and Saucer, sage green (dip), *"Classical Figures,"* mark: WEDGWOOD, 18th century, 3" diameter (saucer). *Courtesy of Skinner, Inc., Boston and Bolton, Ma.* $900-1100.

Cup and Saucer (Trophy), pale blue (solid), mark: WEDGWOOD, ca. 1790, 2.25" x 5.25. ". *Courtesy of the Buten Collection of Wedgwood at the Sands Point Preserve, Sands Point, N.Y.* $1200-1500.

Pair of Cups and Saucers, dark blue (dip), mark: WEDGWOOD, 18th century, 5.25" diameter (saucers). *Courtesy of Skinner, Inc., Boston and Bolton, Ma.* $1500-1800.

Coffee Can and Saucer, lilac (dip, with lapidary polished interior), mark: WEDGWOOD 3, ca. 1790, 2.25" x 2.75". *Courtesy of Ellen Rubell.* $1200-1500.

Coffee Can and Saucer, diceware (dip, lilac and sage green quatrefoils), mark: WEDGWOOD, ca. 1800, 2.25" x 3". *Courtesy of Ellen Rubell.* $1200-1500.

Tea Bowl and Saucer, lilac (dip, with lapidary polished interior), mark: WEDGWOOD 3, ca. 1790, 1,75" x 3". *Courtesy of Ellen Rubell.* $1200-1500.

Coffee Can and Saucer, dark blue (dip), *"Coriolanus,"* mark: WEDGWOOD, ca. 1800, 5.125" diameter (saucer). *Courtesy of Skinner, Inc., Boston and Bolton, Ma.* $1000-1200.

Coffee Can and Saucer, tricolor (dip, black and dark blue), *"Classical Figures,"* mark: WEDGWOOD, early 19th century, 3" h. *Courtesy of Skinner, Inc., Boston and Bolton, Ma.* $2000-4000.

Coffee Can and Saucer (Trophy), tricolor (solid, pale blue and lilac), mark: WEDGWOOD, ca. 1860, 2.5" x 5.25". *Courtesy of the Kerner Collection.* $800-1000.

Coffee Can and Saucer, pale lilac (dip), mark: WEDGWOOD, ca. 1840, 2.5" x 4.5". *Courtesy of the Buten Collection of Wedgwood at the Sands Point Preserve, Sands Point, N.Y.* $800-1000.

Coffee Can and Saucer, dark blue (dip), *"Classical Figures,"* mark: WEDGWOOD, ca. 1860, 2.5" X 5.25". *Courtesy of the Kerner Collection.* $800-1000.

Coffee Can and Saucer, diceware (dip, black with yellow quatrefoils), mark: WEDGWOOD, mid-19th century, 2.5" x 5". *Courtesy of Skinner, Inc., Boston and Bolton, Ma.* $1800-2000.

Coffee Can and Saucer (Trophy), tricolor (dip, sage green and lilac), mark: WEDGWOOD XCD = 1875, 2.5" x 5.25". *Courtesy of the Kerner Collection.* $1000-1200.

Coffee Can and Saucer, sage green (dip), *"Dancing Hours,"* mark: WEDGWOOD, ca. 1890, 2.875" x 5". *Courtesy of the Kerner Collection.* $1000-1200.

Coffee Can and Saucer, tricolor (solid, white with lilac and sage green relief), mark: WEDGWOOD, ALF = 1877, 2.5" x 5.5". *Courtesy of the Esme Wedgwood Collection at the Sands Point Preserve, Sands Point, N.Y.* $1000-1500.

Cup and Saucer, diceware (dip, sage green with yellow quatrefoils), mark: WEDGWOOD, ENGLAND, ca. 1900, 2.5" x 5.375". *Courtesy of Skinner, Inc., Boston and Bolton, Ma.* $1500-1800.

Coffee Can and Saucer, tricolor (solid, white with sage green and lilac relief), mark: WEDGWOOD, mid-19th century, 2.625" h. (can), *Courtesy of Skinner, Inc., Boston and Bolton, Ma.* $1500-1800.

h. Dining Miscellanea

This very broad category encompasses a variety of shapes that are all associated with dining. Their types are listed in the captions and their functions should be self-explanatory. They are arranged alphabetically by type and then further sorted chronologically. Once again the items range from the highly ornamented types that were always meant for display only to the more obviously useful pieces that were definitely meant to be put to work in both elegant and not-so-elegant settings. Shown here are pieces manufactured from the end of the eighteenth century to the end of the twentieth.

Coffee Can and Saucer, sage green (dip), *"Dancing Hours,"* mark: WEDGWOOD, MADE IN ENGLAND, 1989 (reproduction of a classic design), 2.5" x 5". *Courtesy of the Kerner Collection.* $500-600.

Two Demitasse Cups and Saucers, Portland blue and pink (solid), *"Dancing Hours,"* marks: WEDGWOOD, MADE IN ENGLAND, 1992 and 1995, 2.125" x 4.25". *Courtesy of the Kerner Collection.* $100-200 (each).

Apricot Brandy Bottle, sage green (dip), *"Muses,"* mark: WEDGWOOD, 1913 (made for Humphrey Taylor & Co.), 6.75" x 6.5". *Author's Collection.* $400-500.

Butter Dish, pale blue (solid), *"Cupids Drawn by Lions,"* mark: WEDGWOOD, ca. 1790, 4" x 4.75". *Courtesy of Edward L. Knowles.* $1800-2000.

Butter Dish, pale blue (dip, with engine turning on cover), *"Boys at Play,"* mark: WEDGWOOD, ca. 1800, 5" x 7.5". *Courtesy of Jeffrey S. Milkins.* $1300-1500.a

Butter Dish, pale blue (solid), mark: WEDGWOOD, ca 1790, 4.675" w. *Courtesy of Skinner, Inc., Boston and Bolton, Ma.* $900-1100.

Butter Dish, tricolor (dip, sage green and yellow lattice work ornamentation with silver plate mount, lid and handle), mark: WEDGWOOD DJK = 1882, 5.75" x 2.5". *Anonymous Private Collection.* $1000-1200.

Butter Dish, sage green (dip), "Aescalapius Treating a Youth," mark: WEDGWOOD, ca. 1890. 8" x 7" x 3.5. *Courtesy of Julie and Lance Pearce.* $700-800.

Butter Dish, tricolor (dip, dark blue and pale blue with silver plated metal cover), "Sacrifice Figures," mark: WEDGWOOD, ENGLAND, ca. 1900, 2" x 5.5". *Anonymous Private Collection.* $700-800.

Condensed Milk Can Holder with Underplate, dark blue (dip), *"Apollo,"* mark: WEDGWOOD, ENGLAND, ca. 1900, 5.5" x 7". *Author's Collection.* $400-500.

Cheese Dome, lilac (dip), "Sacrifice Figures," mark: WEDGWOOD, IMX = 1869, 12" x 7.5". *Courtesy of Ellen Rubell.* $1800-2000.

Cruet Set, tricolor (dip, dark blue with yellow lattice work ornamentation), mark: WEDGWOOD, ca. 1880, 2.25" x 1.5" (mustard and pepper), 1.5" x 2" (salt cellar). *Courtesy of Adele Ierubino Barnett.* $600-700.

Cheese Dome, pale blue (solid), *"Dancing Hours,"* mark: WEDGWOOD, MADE IN ENGLAND, 1987, 8.25" x 9.5". *Courtesy of the Kerner Collection.* $500-700.

Comma or Custard Cup, pale blue (solid, with lattice work ornamentation, mark: WEDGWOOD, ca. 1785, 1.5" x 2". *Courtesy of Drs. Elaine and Jeffrey Tulman.* $1200-1500.

Custard Cup, pale blue (solid with lattice work ornamentation), mark: WEDGWOOD, 18th century, 2.5" h. *Courtesy of Skinner, Inc., Boston and Bolton, Ma.* $1000-1200.

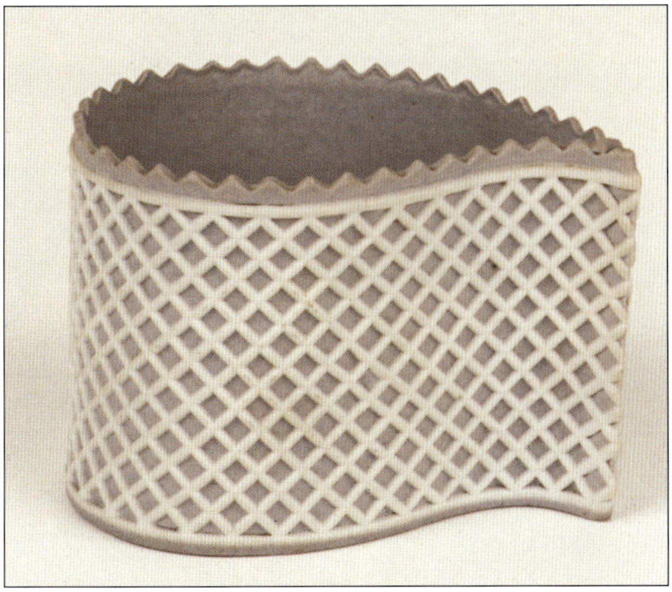

Comma or Custard Cup, lilac (solid, with lattice work ornamentation), mark: WEDGWOOD, ca. 1790, 1.75" x 2.5". *Courtesy of Ellen Rubell.* $1200-1500.

Custard Cup, lilac (dip, with engine turning), mark: WEDGWOOD, ca. 1800, 5" x 4". *Courtesy of Ellen Rubell.* $1500-1700.

Egg Cup, pale blue (solid), *"Cupid,"* mark: WEDGWOOD, ca. 1795, 2.25" x 1.75". *Anonymous Private Collection.* $1000-1200.

Egg Cup, medium blue (solid, with lapidary polished interior), mark: WEDGWOOD, ca. 1790, 2.5" x 1.75". *Courtesy of Dr. and Mrs. Victor Polikoff.* $800-1000.

Egg Cup Holder and Salt Cellar, sage green (dip), "Cupid as Oracle," etc., mark: WEDGWOOD, ca.1890, 6.5" x 3". *Courtesy of Julie and Lance Pearce.* $600-700.

Honey Pot, dark blue (dip), *"Sacrifice Figures,"* mark: WEDGWOOD, ca. 1805, 4.25" x 5". *Courtesy of the Buten Collection of Wedgwood at the Sands Point Preserve, Sands Point, N.Y.* $1000-1200.

Egg Cup, yellow (solid, with black relief), mark: WEDGWOOD, ca. 1820, 2.25" x 1.5". *Courtesy of Dr. and Mrs. Victor Polikoff.* $600-800.

Honey Pot, pale blue (solid), designed for R.B. Willson, Inc., New York, N.Y., mark: WEDGWOOD, MADE IN ENGLAND, 1960. 4.75" x 4.5". *Courtesy of the Buten Collection of Wedgwood at the Sands Point Preserve, Sands Point, N.Y.* $400-500.

Liqueur Bottle, sage green (dip), *"Euterpe,"* Made for and stamped on bottom Humphrey Taylor and Co., London 1770, mark: WEDGWOOD, ca. 1910, 10.5" x 5.5". *Courtesy of David Kroun.* $500-600.

Keg, dark blue (dip, with silver mounts, base and spigot), *"Zephyrs,"* mark: WEDGWOOD (with oval "O" indicating modeled by Bert Bentley), ca. 1900, 6" x 4.5. *Anonymous Private Collection.* $2500-3500.

Marmalade Jar (Footed), tricolor (dip, sage green and lilac with silver plated mount), *"Sportive Love," etc.*, mark: WEDGWOOD, late 19th century, 3.75" h. *Courtesy of Skinner, Inc., Boston and Bolton, Ma.* $700-900.

Muffiner, pale blue (dip). *"Sacrifice Figures,"* mark: WEDGWOOD, ENGLAND, ca. 1900, 8" x 5". *Courtesy of Norm and Romaine Jacobs.* $500-600.

Marmalade Jar (Footed), dark blue (dip, with silver plated mount), *"Aurora," etc*, mark: WEDGWOOD, ETRURIA, ENGLAND, ca. 1895, 3.75" x 4.25". *Courtesy of the Kerner Collection.* $300-400.

Mustard Pot, dark blue (dip, with silver plated mount and cover), *"Three Graces,"* mark: WEDGWOOD, ENGLAND, ca. 1900, 2.5" x 2.25". *Author's Collection.* $250-350.

Mustard, dark blue (dip, with silver plated mount and lid), *"The Procession,"* mark: WEDGWOOD, ENGLAND, ca. 1900, 2.5" x 2.25". *Courtesy of the Kerner Collection.* $150-250.

Napkin Holder, black (dip), *"Dancing Hours,"* mark: WEDGWOOD, ENGLAND, ca. 1900, 2.5" x 1.75". *Courtesy of David Kroun.* $700-800.

Pepper Pot (Upright), dark blue (dip, with silver plated cover), *"The Procession,"* mark: WEDGWOOD, ca. 1890, 3.5" x 2.5". *Author's Collection.* $150-250.

Pêche Melba, black (solid), mark: WEDGWOOD, ca. 1900, 4.5" x 7". *Courtesy of the Kerner Collection.* $1000-1200.

Pepper Pot, dark blue (dip, with silver plated cover), *"Three Graces,"* mark: WEDGWOOD, ENGLAND, ca. 1900, 2.75" x 2". *Author's Collection.* $150-250.

Set of Place Card Holders in Box, various colors (dip), mark: WEDGWOOD, ca. 1900, *Courtesy of Elizabeth and Paul Lauer.* $1500-1800.

Rum Kettle, dark blue (dip) with star and fern pattern, mark: WEDGWOOD, ca. 1840, 6"(not including handle) x 7.5". *Courtesy of the Buten Collection of Wedgwood at the Sands Point Preserve, Sands Point, N.Y.* $1500-2500.

Preserve Jar (Upright), dark blue (dip), *"Sacrifice Figures,"* mark: WEDGWOOD, MADE IN ENGLAND, ca. 1920, 4.5" x 3.5". *Author's Collection.* $200-300.

Rum Kettle, dark blue (dip, with silver plated mount), *"Sacrifice to Ceres,"* mark: WEDGWOOD, 6" h. . *Courtesy of Skinner, Inc., Boston and Bolton, Ma.* $800-1000.

Rum Kettle, pale blue (solid), *"Dancing Hours,"* mark: WEDGWOOD, MADE IN ENGLAND, 1993 (Limited Edition in 'Wedgwood Heritage Series' based on an 18th century original), 9" x 8.5". *Courtesy of the Kerner Collection.* $800-1000.

Salt Shaker (Etruscan), dark blue (dip), "Three Graces," mark: WEDGWOOD, ca. 1890, 3" x 1.75". *Courtesy of David Kroun.* $300-400.

Salt Cellar, pale blue (solid), *"Boys at Play,"* mark: WEDGWOOD, ca. 1790, 1.75" x 3.25". *Courtesy of the Kerner Collection.* $1000-1200.

Pair of Salt Cellars, dark blue (dip, with silver plated mounts and spoons in original box), mark: WEDGWOOD, ca. 1900, 1.5" x 2.5" (each salt cellar), *Courtesy of Drs. Elaine and Jeffrey Tulman.* $800-1000.

Salt Cellar, pale blue (solid, with lapidary polished interior), mark: WEDGWOOD, eighteenth century, 2.75" w. *Courtesy of Skinner, Inc., Boston and Bolton, Ma.* $1500-1800.

Salt Cellar, dark blue (dip, with silver plated mount), *"Cupids at Play,"* mark: WEDGWOOD, ENGLAND, ca. 1900, 1.75" x 2.25". *Author's Collection*. $150-250.

Sauce Boat, pale blue (solid), mark: WEDGWOOD, 18th century, 9.5" w. *Courtesy of Skinner, Inc., Boston and Bolton, Ma.* $1800-2000.

Salt Cellar (Upright), dark blue (dip, with silver plated mount), *"Cupids at Play,"* mark: WEDGWOOD, ENGLAND, ca. 1900, 1.5" x 2.25". *Author's Collection*. $150-250.

Tankard, pale blue (solid), *"Domestic Employment,"* mark: WEDGWOOD, 18th century, 6" h. *Courtesy of Skinner, Inc., Boston and Bolton, Ma.* $1200-1500.

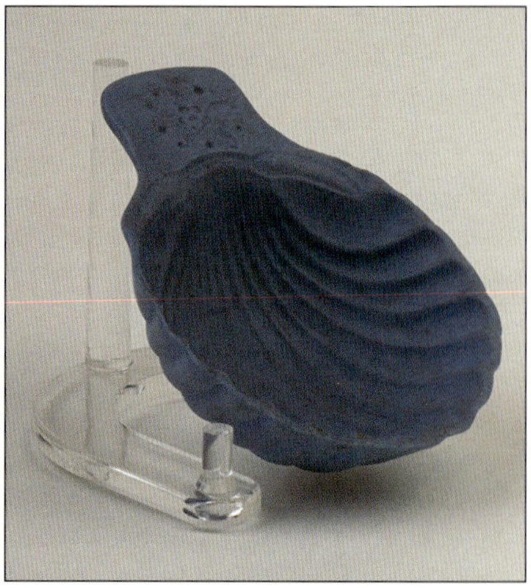

Tea Caddy Spoon, pale blue (solid), mark: Wedgwood (unusual upper and lower case mark), ca. 1790, 2" x 1.25". *Courtesy of Drs. Elaine and Jeffrey Tulman*. $1100-1300.

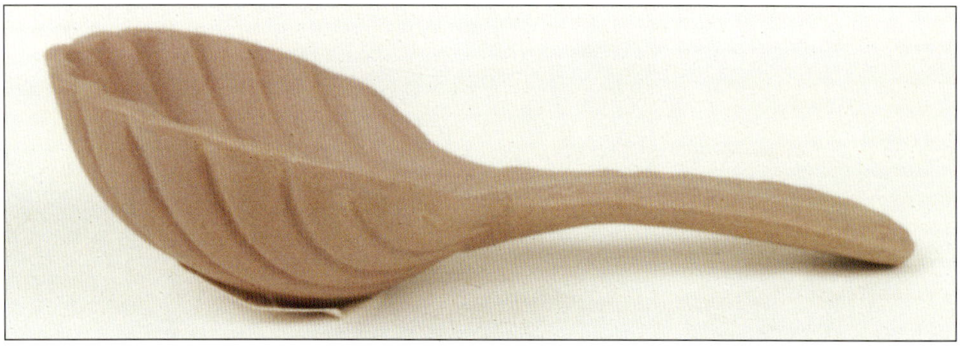

Tea Caddy Spoon, lilac (solid), mark: WEDGWOOD, ca. 1820, 5.25" x 1.75". *Courtesy of Ellen Rubell.* $800-900.

Trembleuse or Chocolate Cup, sage green (dip, with engine turning), mark: WEDGWOOD, 18th century, 4.5" h. *Courtesy of Skinner, Inc., Boston and Bolton, Ma.* $1200-1500.

Tea Canister, dark blue (dip), mark: WEDGWOOD WIO = 1860 or 1886, 5.25" x 3". *Author's Collection.* $500-600.

Trembleuse or Chocolate Cup and Saucer, diceware (dip, sage green and yellow quatrefoils with lotus finial), mark: WEDGWOOD, mid-19th century, 3" x 5.25". *Courtesy of Skinner, Inc., Boston and Bolton, Ma.* $1500-1800.

Tea Canister, olive green (dip), *"Benjamin Franklin,"* mark: WEDGWOOD, ENGLAND, ca. 1930 (design originally produced for American Centennial in 1876), 5.5" x 3". *Anonymous Private Collection.* $700-800.

Wine Cooler with Swan Handles, diceware (dip, sage green with yellow quatrefoils), *"Roman Banquet,"* mark: Wedgwood (rare upper and lower case), ca. 1790. 12" x 7". *Courtesy of Leo Kaplan, Ltd. NYC.* $10,000-12,000.

Wine Cooler, dark blue (dip) with silver plated rim and handle, mark: WEDGWOOD, ca. 1880. *Courtesy of Adele Ierubino Barnett.* $400-500.

i. Figures

Figures of various types have been made in Jasper from Josiah Wedgwood's time to the present day. Only a small selection is shown here but it encompasses some superbly artistic examples from various periods. The Sphinx and Somnus figures are highly sought after icons of early Wedgwood at its best. In recent decades many figures have been produced in "large limited editions" (to use an oxymoron) for the collectors market of which the Dancing Hours figure is a prime example. Other figure series include the Muses and the Herculaneum Dancers.

Sphinx Figure (Paperweight?), dark blue and white (dip), mark: WEDGWOOD, eighteenth century, 6.5" l. *Courtesy of Skinner, Inc., Boston and Bolton, Ma.* $3000-5000.

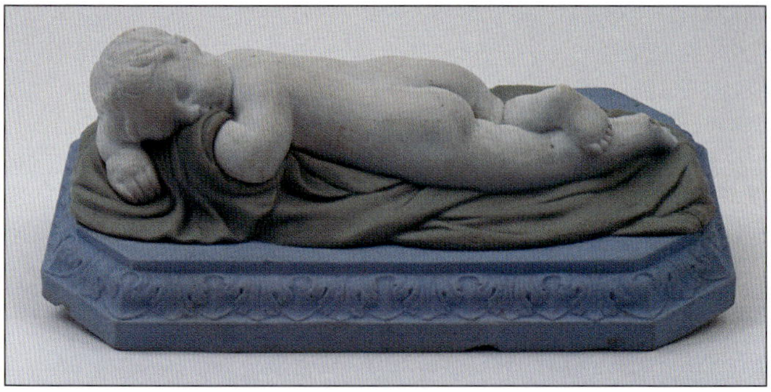

Somnus (Sleeping Boy), tricolor (solid, white, pale blue and sage green), mark: WEDGWOOD, ca. 1800, 3.75" x 5". *Courtesy of Dr. and Mrs. Victor Polikoff.* $7000-9000.

Figure on Base, pale blue and white (solid), *"Cupid,"* mark: WEDGWOOD, ca. 1790, 7.5" x 3". *Anonymous Private Collection.* $7500-9500.

Figure on Base, pale blue and white (solid), *"Ganymede and the Eagle,"* mark: Wedgwood (unusual upper and lower case mark), ca. 1790, 7" x 3". *Courtesy of Drs. Elaine and Jeffrey Tulman*. $4000-5000.

Figure, white (solid), *"Jean Jacques Rousseau,"* mark: WEDDGWOOD, ca. 1790, 10.5" x 3". *Courtesy of Drs. Elaine and Jeffrey Tulman.* $5000-6000.

Figure, pale blue and white (solid), *"Dancing Hour,"* mark: WEDGWOOD, MADE IN ENGLAND, 1997 ("limited" edition of 12,500), 10.5" x 7". *Courtesy of the Kerner Collection.* $200-300.

Taurus, terra cotta (solid, modeled by Arnold Machin), mark: WEDGWOOD, MADE IN ENGLAND, 1957, 15" x 6". *Anonymous Private Collection.* $700-800.

j. Inkwells

Before there were computers or even ballpoint pens, it was necessary to have a supply of ink in order to commit pen to paper. Going back to the days of the Wedgwood and Bentley partnership, inkwells have always been produced by the Company in a variety of styles. The small selection shown here displays quite a diverse group including both simple and elaborate Jasper designs all of which are avidly pursued by both Wedgwood and inkwell collectors alike. It can easily be said that at the present time, except for legions of collectors, inkwells have become as extinct as woolly mammoths.

Inkwell and Candle Holder, pale blue (solid), mark: WEDGWOOD, eighteenth century, 3.375" h. *Courtesy of Skinner, Inc., Boston and Bolton, Ma.* $1000-1200.

Inkstand and Inkwells (covers missing), pale blue (solid), *"Marriage of Cupid and Psyche,"* mark: WEDGWOOD, ca. 1795, 6.25" x 6.25". *Courtesy of the Buten Collection of Wedgwood at the Sands Point Preserve, Sands Point, N.Y.* $1500-1800.

Inkstand (covers missing), pale blue (solid), *"Sacrifice to Hymen,"* mark: WEDGWOOD, ca. 1795, 6.875" h. *Courtesy of Skinner, Inc., Boston and Bolton, Ma.* $1500-1800.

Inkwells on Stand, dark blue (dip), 3" x 8". mark: WEDGWOOD, ca. 1860, *Author's Collection.* $1000-1200.

Details of previous item *"Marcus Curtius"* and *"Day and Night."*.

Inkwell, pale blue (dip) + brass mountings, "Nike and the Warrior," mark: WEDG-WOOD, BUU = 1866, 2.75" x 2.75". *Courtesy of Julie and Lance Pearce.* $600-700.

Inkwell (including insert and underplate), pale blue (dip), "Muses Watering Pegasus, " etc., mark: Wedgwood, XDC = 1874, 6.5" x 3". *Courtesy of Adele Ierubino Barnett.* $650-750.

Inkwell with glass insert, sage green (dip), *"Dipping of Achilles,"* mark: WEDGWOOD, ca. 1885, 3.25" x 3.25". *Anonymous Private Collection.* $600-800.

Inkwell, dark blue (dip, with silver plate cover), mark: WEDGWOOD, ca. 1890, 2" x 3.25". *Anonymous Private Collection.* $500-700.

k. Jewelry

Jewelry made from Wedgwood Jasper has a history that goes back to the eighteenth century. As medallions with bas-reliefs were made in the style of earlier types of cameos made from stones or shells, it was only natural that they would be mounted in metal for rings, pendants, brooches, earrings and other types of jewelry. At times a piece of Wedgwood Jasper jewelry can consist of a medallion with a contemporary setting, while, more often than not, a much older medallion will be found in a more modern setting. Metals used for mounting can be cut steel, in very early examples, various grades of gold, silver and ormolu. Wedgwood Jasper jewelry is still being produced and can be purchased at the various Waterford Wedgwood stores. Both antique and modern examples are very highly collectible with price tags that go from very affordable to quite expensive. Older items made from tricolor medallions are especially sought after.

Bracelet, pale blue (solid) in sterling silver mounts, "Cupids" and other Classical Figures, mark: WEDGWOOD, ca. 1890, 7" long. *Courtesy of Naomi Herman*. $350-450.

Brooch, black (solid, in gold setting), *"Perseus and Andromeda."* mark: WEDGWOOD & BENTLEY, ca. 1775, 1.25" x 1". *Courtesy of Drs. Elaine and Jeffrey Tulman*. $1500-2000.

Brooch, tricolor doublet (dark blue and lilac) in platinum and gold mount with diamonds and seed pearls, mark: none visible, ca. 1780, 1" x 0.75". *Courtesy of Dr. and Mrs. Victor Polikoff*. $4500-5500.

Brooch, pale blue (solid) mounted in bronze, "Cupid Stringing his Bow," mark: not visible, ca. 1790, 2" x 1.5". *Courtesy of the Buten Collection of Wedgwood at the Sands Point Preserve, Sands Point, N.Y.* $800-1000.

Brooch, pale blue (solid) in mounted in gold, *"Sacrifice to Hymen,"* mark: not visible, ca. 1790, 2" x 1.5". *Courtesy of the Buten Collection of Wedgwood at the Sands Point Preserve, Sands Point, N.Y.* $800-1200.

Brooch, white (solid, with gilded relief in gold setting), *"Cupid Market,"* mark: WEDGWOOD, ca. 1800, 1.25" x 1". *"Courtesy of Drs. Elaine and Jeffrey Tulman.* $800-1000.

Brooch, tricolor (dip, sage green and pale blue in gold mount), *"Cupids and Lions,"* mark: WEDGWOOD, early 19th century, 1" x 1.25". *Courtesy of Skinner, Inc., Boston and Bolton, Ma.* $600-800.

Brooch, tricolor (dip, yellow and black) in 14k gold mount, *"A Sacrifice,"* mark: WEDGWOOD, ca. 1810, 1.5" x 1.25". *Courtesy of Naomi Herman.* $800-1000.

Brooch, tricolor (dark blue and sage green), *"Sacrifice Figures,"* mark: WEDGWOOD, ca. 1810. 2.25" x .75". *Courtesy of Marilyn and Norm McClennan. $600-700.*

Brooch, dark blue (dip) in 9kt gold mount, *"Sacrifice to Ceres?,"* mark: WEDGWOOD, ca. 1880, 1.5" x 1.25", *Courtesy of Naomi Herman.* $400-500.

Brooch/Pendant, tricolor (dip, pale blue and sage green) in 14k gold mount, *"Nike,"* mark: WEDGWOOD, ca. 1810, 1.5" diameter. *Courtesy of Naomi Herman.* $650-750.

Brooch, dark blue (dip), *"Sacrifice Figures,"* mark: WEDGWOOD, ca. 1890, 1.25" diameter. *Courtesy of Naomi Herman.* $250-350.

Brooch/Pendant, tricolor (dip, sage green and dark blue) in 9k gold mount, *"Sacrifice Figure,"* mark: WEDGWOOD, ca. 1880, 1.5" x 1.5". *Courtesy of Naomi Herman.* $450-550.

Brooch, dark blue (solid) in 9kt gold mount, *"Cupid Disarmed"* mark: WEDGWOOD, ca. 1890, 1" x 0.5". *Courtesy of Naomi Herman.* $200-300.

Earrings, dark blue (solid) with 14kt gold mounts, *"Classical Figures,"* mark: none visible, ca. 1800, 2.5" x 0.75". *Courtesy of Terry Rodgers & Melody.* $2000-3000.

Brooch/Pendant, dark blue (solid) in 9kt gold mount, *"Cupids and Lions,"* mark: WEDGWOOD, ca. 1890, 1" x 0.75". *Courtesy of Naomi Herman.* $200-300.

Pendant, dark blue (dip) in 9k gold mount, *"Marine Venus,"* mark: WEDGWOOD, ca. 1890, 1.5" x 1.25". *Courtesy of Naomi Herman.* $400-500.

Chatelaine, dark blue (solid) in cut steel mount, *"Classical Figures,"* mark: none visible, ca. 1780, 10" long. *Courtesy of Dr. and Mrs. Victor Polikoff.* $5000-7000.

Pendant, sage green (solid) in 9kt gold mount, *"Classical Warrior,"* mark: WEDGWOOD, ca. 1890, 0.75" x 0.25". *Courtesy of Naomi Herman.* $200-300.

Pendant, pale blue (solid) in sterling silver mount, *"Cleopatra,"* mark: WEDGWOOD, ca. 1890, 0.75" diameter. *Courtesy of Naomi Herman.* $150-250.

Ring, tricolor (dip, lilac and dark blue) in 9kt gold mount, *"Classical Figure,"* mark: WEDGWOOD, ca. 1810, 0.75" x 0.5". *Courtesy of Naomi Herman.* $450-550.

Ring, black (solid) in 14k gold mount, *"Sacrifice Figure,"* mark: WEDGWOOD, ca. 1880, 1" x 0.75". *Courtesy of Naomi Herman.* $400-500.

Pendant, dark blue (dip) in sterling silver mount, *"Apollo Musagetes,"* mark: WEDGWOOD, ca. 1890, 1.75" x 1". *Courtesy of Naomi Herman.* $250-350.

Ring, dark blue (solid) in 14k gold mount, *"Classical Figure,"* mark: WEDGWOOD, ca. 1890. 0.5" x 0.25". *Courtesy of Naomi Herman.* $300-400.

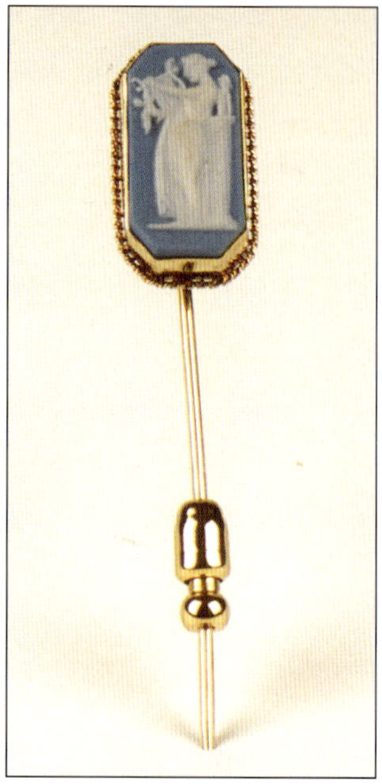

Stick Pin, pale blue (solid) in 10k gold mount, *"Classical Figure with Lyre,"* mark: WEDGWOOD, ca. 1890, 0.75" x 0.3725". *Courtesy of Naomi Herman.* $150-250.

Two Pendants, tricolor (solid) in 14k gold mounts,: (1) pale and Royal blue; (2)terracotta and black, *"Floral Girl" and "Three Graces,"* mark: WEDGWOOD, MADE IN ENGLAND, 1979, 1.25" x 1" and 1.25" diameter. *Courtesy of Naomi Herman.* $150-250 (each).

1. Jugs and Mugs

Jugs and mugs are among the most commonly seen categories of Wedgwood Jasper. They have been produced in a vast array of shapes, styles, colors, and sizes since the earliest years of Jasper. They vary from such splendid examples as the elaborately shaped and decorated wine ewers, water ewers, and oenoechoes, to the more mundane types of jugs and mugs with modest to sparse ornamentation. The Upright, the Etruscan, the Dutch, and the Orange shape jugs are the most consistently found as they have been steadily produced over the last two centuries. Judging by what is offered for sale on eBay, the Upright, popularly known as the rope-handled jug, is probably the most ubiquitous of all Wedgwood Jasper items larger than an ashtray. The Etruscan shape has always been very popular among collectors and some modern versions shown here are examples of the Wedgwood Company making a strong effort to cater to this audience. On the other hand, jugs and mugs have also been made over the years as useful items with metal lids of silver plate or pewter. Obviously, what distinguishes jugs from mugs is that the former is made for pouring while the latter is made for drinking. Thus the mugs lack a spout.

Water and Wine Ewers, pale blue (solid), "Sacred to Neptune," and "Sacred to Bacchus," mark: WEDGWOOD, ca. 1785. 15" x 6.5". *Anonymous Private Collection.* $15,000-20,000.

Wine Ewer, black (dip), mark: WEDGWOOD and inscribed "J. Sidebotham, July 6, 1882," 16" h. *Courtesy of Skinner, Inc., Boston and Bolton, Ma.* $1200-1500.

Jug (Turned), pale blue (solid), *"Domestic Employment,"* mark: Wedgwood (rare upper and lower case), 12" h. *Courtesy of Leo Kaplan, Ltd. NYC.* $8000-10,000.

Jug (Turned), diceware (dip, dark blue with sage green quatrefoils), mark: WEDGWOOD, ca. 1790, 5.5" x 4.5". *Courtesy of Drs. Elaine and Jeffrey Tulman.* $4000-5000.

Jug (Oenochoe), pale blue (solid), mark: WEDGWOOD, ca. 1870, 7.75" x 3". *Courtesy of the Kerner Collection.* $700-900.

Jug (Club), medium blue (dip), *"Bacchanalian Boys at Play,"* mark: WEDGWOOD, ca. 1820, 7.5" x 6.25". *Courtesy of Edward L. Knowles.* $1500-1800.

Jug (Miniature), dark blue (dip), *"Classical Figures,"* mark: WEDGWOOD, ca. 1870, 1.5" x 1.25". *Courtesy of Sarah Marie White*. $400-500.

Jug, sage green (dip), "*Sacrifice Figures*," mark: WEDGWOOD, ENGLAND, ca. 1895, 5" x 5". *Courtesy of Mary and Peter Rockefeller.* $300-400.

Jug (Etruscan), tricolor (solid, white with sage green and lilac relief), mark: WEDGWOOD, ca. 1880, 7" x 5". *Courtesy of Mary and Peter Rockefeller.* $700-800.

Jug, lilac (dip), *"Terpsichore" and "Clio,"* mark: WEDGWOOD, ENGLAND, 1891, 4" x 3". *Courtesy of Ellen Rubell.* $500-600.

Jug (Dutch), white (solid, with sage green and lilac relief), mark: WEDGWOOD, ca. 1880, 5.5" x 6.25". *Anonymous Private Collection.* $1200-1500.

Pair of Jugs (Etruscan), yellow (dip), *"Offering to Peace" and "Sacrifice Figures,"* marks: WEDGWOOD, ENGLAND, ca. 1900, 5.25" x 4.5" and 8" x 6.5". *Courtesy of Edward L. Knowles.* $2000-2500.

Jug (Dutch), white (solid) with sage green relief, *"Sacrifice Figures,"* mark: WEDGWOOD, ENGLAND, ca 1900, 5" x 6". *Anonymous Private Collection.* $600-700.

Jug (Upright), tricolor (dip, sage green and yellow lattice work ornamentation with silver plate mount and lid), mark: WEDGWOOD DJR = 1863 or 1869, 7.5" x 4.5". *Anonymous Private Collection.* $1200-1500.

Jug (Upright), tricolor (dip, dark blue with yellow lattice work ornamentation), mark: WEDGWOOD, ca. 1880, 7.25" x 4.25". . *Courtesy of Jeffrey S. Milkins.* $800-1000.

Jug (1016), dark blue (dip), mark: WEDGWOOD, ca. 1890, 6.5" x 5". *Anonymous Private Collection.* $500-600.

Jug, dark blue (dip, with silver plated lid), *"Offering to Peace,"* mark: WEDGWOOD, ca. 1890, 5.5" x 6.25". *Author's Collection.* $250-350.

Jug (Upright), dark blue (dip), "Caperns Birds," mark WEDG-WOOD, MADE IN ENGLAND and CAPERNS, LTD., BRISTOL, 1934, 6" x 4.5. *Courtesy of Dr. and Mrs. Victor Polikoff.* $300-400.

Two Jugs (Upright), yellow buff (dip) with black relief, yellow (dip), *"Sacrifice Figures" and "Offering to Peace,"* marks: WEDG-WOOD, MADE IN ENGLAND, ca. 1930 and WEDGWOOD, ENGLAND, ca. 1900, 6.5" x 4.5". *Courtesy of Dr. and Mrs. Victor Polikoff.* $600-800 and $800-1000.

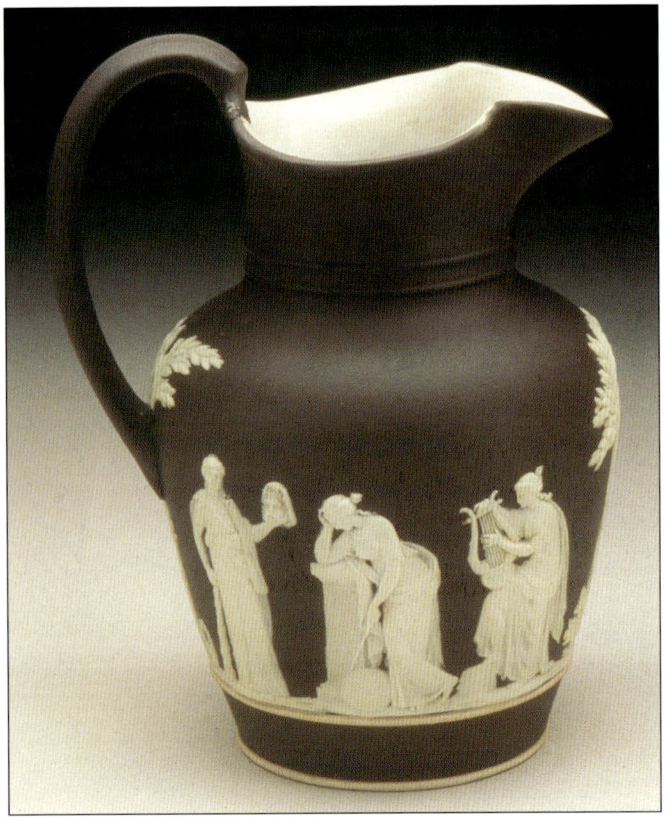

Jug (Club), Chocolate Brown (dip), *"Muses,"* mark: WEDG-WOOD, 19th century, 7" h. *Courtesy of Skinner, Inc., Boston and Bolton, Ma.* $900-1100.

Jug (Etruscan), crimson (dip), *"Sacrifice Figures,"* mark: WEDG-WOOD, ENGLAND, 4.75" h. *Courtesy of Skinner, Inc., Boston and Bolton, Ma.* $1200-1500.

Jug (Covered), sage green (dip), *"Dipping of Achilles,"* mark: WEDGWOOD, mid-19th century, 6" h. *Courtesy of Skinner, Inc., Boston and Bolton, Ma.* $600-800.

Jug (Etruscan), primrose (solid, with taupe relief), *"Sacrifice Figures,"* mark: WEDGWOOD, MADE IN ENGLAND®, 1989, 5.5" x 4.5". *Courtesy of David Kroun.* $400-500.

Jug (Etruscan), tricolor (solid, teal with primrose and terracotta relief), *"Sacrifice Figures,"* mark: WEDGWOOD, MADE IN ENGLAND, ca. 1985, 5.5" x 4.5". *Courtesy of David Kroun.* $500-600.

Jug (Etruscan), tricolor (solid, Portland blue with pale blue and sage green relief), *"Sacrifice Figures,"* mark: WEDGWOOD, MADE IN ENGLAND, ca. 1985, 5.5" x 4.5". *Courtesy of David Kroun.* $500-600.

Jug (Etruscan), tricolor (solid, pale blue with primrose and terracotta relief), *"Sacrifice Figures,"* mark: WEDGWOOD, MADE IN ENGLAND, 1986, 5" x 4". *Courtesy of Elizabeth and Paul Lauer.* $300-400.

Mug, slate blue, *"Boys at Play,"* mark: WEDGWOOD, ca. 1790, 3.25" x 3". *Courtesy of Elizabeth and Paul Lauer.* $800-1000.

Mug (Upright with Harry Barnard motto design), olive green (dip), Motto: *"No Man Does Ill that Liveth Well,"* mark: WEDGWOOD, ENGLAND, ca. 1930, 5.25" x 5. *Courtesy of Jeffrey S. Milkins.* $1000-1200.

Mug (Upright with Harry Barnard motto Design), dark blue (dip), Motto: *"Drinke Faire, Don't Sware,"* mark: WEDGWOOD, ENGLAND, ca. 1900, 5.25" h. *Courtesy of Skinner, Inc., Boston and Bolton, Ma.* $500-700.

Mug (Upright with Harry Barnard motto design), sage green (dip), Motto: *"Who Lives a Good Life is Sure to Live Well,"* mark: WEDGWOOD, ca. 1920, 5.25" h. *Courtesy of Skinner, Inc., Boston and Bolton, Ma.* $800-1000.

Mug (Upright), dark blue (dip) with metal mount, *"Sacrifice Figures,"* mark: WEDGWOOD and ELKINGTON & CO, LTD, ca. 1910 (Issued to Commemorate the National Rifle Association of the U.K.), 5" x 5". *Author's Collection.* $200-300.

Loving Mug or Tyg (Bentley), dark blue (dip), *"Bellerophon Watering Pegasus,"* mark: WEDGWOOD, ENGLAND, ca. 1900, 4.75" x 6". *Anonymous Private Collection.* $800-1000.

Mug (Upright), dark blue (dip), *"King George VI,"* mark: WEDGWOOD, MADE IN ENGLAND, 1939 (Issued to commemorate King's visit to Canada), 4.5" x 5." *Courtesy of Dr. and Mrs. Victor Polikoff.* $350-450.

m. Lamps

The enormously varied group of shapes in this section only have in common their use as lamps. Some were made to be either lamps themselves or bases in which lamps were placed while others have been adapted post-factory to illuminate someone's home. Wedgwood produced the earliest examples of Jasper lamps in 1775. They were modeled after various ancient prototypes that had been unearthed during recent decades. Small, hand held oil lamps were probably the flashlights of their time and were continually made into the late nineteenth century. These original Wedgwood models, however, are greatly outnumbered by lamps that have been fashioned from pre-existing Wedgwood items especially vases and candlesticks. Holes are bored through the bases to allow passage of a wire and a fixture for bulbs is grafted to the top. Many lovely examples have been fashioned in this manner, but one cannot help but regret the "vandalism" involved in this process.

Pair of Lamp Cases, pale blue (solid, with engine turning), *"Blind Man's Buff,"* mark: WEDGWOOD, ca. 1790, 7.125" *Courtesy of Skinner, Inc., Boston and Bolton, Ma.* $2500-3500.

Lamp, sage green (dip, with bronze (?) mounts), *"Marriage of Cupid and Psyche,"* mark: none visible, ca. 1840, 15.25" x 6". *Courtesy of Edward L. Knowles.* $1000-1200.

Pair of Oil Lamps, white (solid), *"Vestal and Reading Figures,"* mark: WEDGWOOD, early 19th century, 8.5" h. *Courtesy of Skinner, Inc., Boston and Bolton, Ma.* $5000-7000.

Lamp Base, dark blue (dip, with brass mounts), *"Portland Vase Frieze,"* mark: none visible, ca. 1840, 10" x 6". *Courtesy of Elizabeth and Paul Lauer.* $1000-1200.

Hand or Oil Lamp, dark blue (dip), *"Psyche Bound to a Tree by Cupids,"* mark: WEDGWOOD, ca. 1820. 1.25" X 4.25". *Courtesy of Jeffrey S. Milkins.* $1000-1200.

Oil Lamp, black (dip), mark: WEDGWOOD, mid-19th century, 5.875" w. *Courtesy of Skinner, Inc., Boston and Bolton, Ma.* $900-1100.

Chandelier, pale blue (dip) in metal mounts, *"Muses,"* , marks: WEDGWOOD, late 19th century, 34" overall h. ". *Courtesy of Skinner, Inc., Boston and Bolton, Ma.* $1800-2000.

Lamp (fashioned from Vase 264), dark blue (dip), "Sportive Love," mark: WEDGWOOD, ca. 1890, 8" x 4.5" (not including shade and base). *Author's Collection.* $400-500.

n. Medallions

Medallions or cameos (which tend to be smaller) were the earliest type of Wedgwood product that were made from Jasper. They can generally be described as small, flat bases of various shapes to which a bas-relief has been applied. They have been and still are employed as decoration for furniture as well as the starting point for pieces of jewelry. Medallions on their own have always been highly collectible and, since the time of Wedgwood and Bentley, they have been continually issued as individual items or in thematic series. Portrait medallions have encompassed everyone from illustrious ancient Greeks and Romans and Josiah Wedgwood's famous contemporaries to all manner of noted personages down to our present day. Classical subjects based on mythology are the other main topic of the medallions and this is basically what is on display here. The medallions can be either solid or dip Jasper and when they have been attached to jewelry or other objects it is often hard to determine just which type they are. Early medallions, made prior to 1800, can be found with lapidary polished edges.

Single Colored

The vast majority of medallions were produced in one color (either solid or dip) with the applied bas-relief in white. Medallions of this type have been continually produced from the eighteenth century through modern times.

Medallion, pale blue (solid), *"Sacrifice Figure,"* mark: WEDGWOOD & BENTLEY, ca. 1775, 3.25" x 2.75". *Courtesy of Drs. Elaine and Jeffrey Tulman*. $1200-1500.

Medallion, pale blue (solid, in frame), *"Hercules,"* mark: WEDGWOOD & BENTLEY, ca. 1775, 2" x 1.5". *Courtesy of Drs. Elaine and Jeffrey Tulman*. $1200-1500.

Medallion, white (solid, with blue inlay), mark (on front): BY J. WEDGWOOD F.R.S., 1784, 1.875" x 1.375". *Courtesy of Dr. and Mrs. Victor Polikoff*. $600-800. (F.R.S. = Fellow of the Royal Society of London for Improving Natural Knowledge to which Wedgwood was elected for his invention of the pyrometer).

Medallion, dark blue (dip on both sides), "Cupids at Play," mark: WEDGWOOD, ca. 1780, 2.75" x 1.25". *Courtesy of Dr. and Mrs. Victor Polikoff*. $1000-1200.

Medallion, dark blue (dip, with lapidary polished edge). *"Zephyr,"* mark: WEDGWOOD, ca. 1790, 2.5" x 1.5". *Courtesy of Drs. Elaine and Jeffrey Tulman*. $900-1000.

Medallion, dark blue (dip, with lapidary polished edge), *"Health is Restored,"* (referring to King George III), mark: WEDGWOOD, 1789, 3" x 1.5". *Courtesy of Drs. Elaine and Jeffrey Tulman*. $900-1000.

Medallion, dark blue (dip, with lapidary polished edge), *"Coronation of Leopold II,"* (one of the "German Cameos"), mark: WEDGWOOD, ca. 1790, 2.75" x 1.5. *Courtesy of Drs. Elaine and Jeffrey Tulman*. $900-1000.

Medallion, dark blue (dip) with lapidary edge, *"Aurora," etc.*, mark: WEDGWOOD, ca. 1795, 2.75" x 1.5". *Courtesy of the Buten Collection of Wedgwood at the Sands Point Preserve, Sands Point, N.Y.* $800-1200.

Multicolored

These stunning little tricolor, four-color and five-color works of art demonstrate Wedgwood workmanship and miniaturization at its best. The classical subjects are beautifully highlighted by the several contrasting colors that they rest upon. While most multicolor medallions date from the late eighteenth and early nineteenth centuries, some have been reproduced in later years including some late twentieth century issues mostly intended for jewelry.

Medallion, tricolor (dip, dark blue and sage green), *"Marcus Scaevola before King Porsena,"* mark: WEDGWOOD, ca. 1790, 2.25" x 1.25". ". *Courtesy of the Buten Collection of Wedgwood at the Sands Point Preserve, Sands Point, N.Y.* $800-1200.

Medallion, bright blue (solid) in metal frame, *"France and Liberty Joining Hands Before a Statue of Plenty,"* mark: Wedgwood, ca. 1800, 2.25" diameter, *Courtesy of the Buten Collection of Wedgwood at the Sands Point Preserve, Sands Point, N.Y.* $1000-1200.

Medallion, tricolor (dip, sage green and dark blue), *"Marcus Scaevola before King Porsena,"* mark: WEDGWOOD, ca. 1790, 2.25" x 1.25". ". *Courtesy of the Buten Collection of Wedgwood at the Sands Point Preserve, Sands Point, N.Y.* $800-1200.

Medallion, tricolor (dip, lilac and dark blue with lapidary polished edge), *"A Sacrifice,"* mark: WEDGWOOD, ca. 1795, 2.25" diameter. *Courtesy of Ellen Rubell.* $800-900.

Three Medallions, tricolor (dip, with lapidary polished edges), from top to bottom: (1) lilac and dark blue, *"Classical Figures,"* 0.625" x 1.875"; (2) sage green and dark blue, *"Classical Figures,"* 0.625" x 2.5"; (3) black and sage green, *"Night and Day,"* 1" x 2.625", marks: WEDGWOOD, eighteenth century. *Courtesy of Skinner, Inc., Boston and Bolton, Ma.* $1000-1200.

Two Medallions, tricolor (dip, with lapidary polished edges), from top to bottom: (1) sage green and dark blue, "Cupids and Lions," 0.875" x 2"; (2)sage green and lilac, *"Classical Figures,"* 1" x 2.125", marks: WEDGWOOD, eighteenth century. *Courtesy of Skinner, Inc., Boston and Bolton, Ma.* $700-800.

Medallion, tricolor (dip, lilac and sage green with lapidary polished edge), *"The Power of Love"* mark: WEDGWOOD, ca. 1795, 2.25" diameter. *Courtesy of Ellen Rubell.* $800-900.

Pair of Medallions, tricolor (dip, lilac and sage green), "Bellerophon Watering Pegasus" and *"Three Graces(?),"* marks: WEDGWOOD, eighteenth century, 2.125" diameter. *Courtesy of Skinner, Inc., Boston and Bolton, Ma.* $1000-1200.

Medallion, five color (dip, lilac, pale blue, yellow and sage green), *"Marcus Scaevola before King Porsena,"* mark: WEDGWOOD, early 19th century, 2.625" w. *Courtesy of Skinner, Inc., Boston and Bolton, Ma.* $1000-1200.

Medallion, four color (dip, sage green, dark blue and lilac), *"Achilles Dragging Hector Around the Walls of Troy,"* mark: WEDGWOOD, ca. 1840, 4.5" x 3". *Courtesy of Dr. and Mrs. Victor Polikoff.* $1500-1800.

Medallion, four color (dip, pale blue, lilac and sage green), *"Cupid Market,"* mark: WEDGWOOD, ca. 1800, 2.625" w. *Courtesy of Skinner, Inc., Boston and Bolton, Ma.* $800-900.

Medallion (diamond shaped), tricolor (solid, white with lilac and sage green relief), *"unknown figure,"* mark: WEDGWOOD, ca. 1870, 1.5" x 2.25". *Courtesy of the Buten Collection of Wedgwood at the Sands Point Preserve, Sands Point, N.Y.* $400-500.

Doublet (two medallions back- to-back), tricolor (dip, dark blue and lilac), *"Diana,"* mark: none visible, ca. 1810, 1" x 0.5". *Courtesy of Naomi Herman.* $300-400.

Medallion (diamond shaped), tricolor, (solid, white with lilac and sage green relief), *"Cupid and Anchor,"* mark:WEDGWOOD, ca. 1870, 2.25" x 1.5". *Courtesy of the Buten Collection of Wedgwood at the Sands Point Preserve, Sands Point, N.Y.* $400-500.

o. Perfume Bottles

Medallion, tricolor (dip, pale blue and lilac), *"Caduceus, Clasped Hands and Cornucopiae,"* mark: WEDGWOOD, ca. 1900, 1.75" x 1.75". *Courtesy of Dr. and Mrs. Victor Polikoff.* $700-900.

Perfume or scent bottles have been produced in Jasper since the eighteenth century and early examples are among the most highly sought after categories of antique Wedgwood. They were offered in a variety of shapes and colors (including tricolor combinations) with simple, but highly striking, neo-classical ornamentation. Many of these early models were reproduced throughout the nineteenth century. Most perfume bottles are unmarked probably because of a lack of space to incise the Wedgwood mark. The bottles came with metal stoppers, though many surviving examples have been fitted with replacements. The several twentieth century examples shown here have rather austere designs and some have atomizer tops to more easily distribute their contents.

Perfume Bottle, pale blue (solid), *"Minerva,"* mark: none visible, ca. 1785, 2.25" x 1.75". *Anonymous Private Collection.* $900-1100.

Two Medallions, tricolor (dip, yellow and sage green/ dip, pale and dark blue), *"Night and Day,"* mark: WEDGWOOD, early 20th century (attributed to Bert Bentley), 2.375" l./3" l. *Courtesy of Skinner, Inc., Boston and Bolton, Ma.* $1000-1200.

Perfume Bottle, tricolor (dip, dark blue and sage green), *"Venus and Cupid,"* mark: none visible, ca. 1790, 3.5" x 1.25". *Anonymous Private Collection.* $3500-4000.

Perfume Bottle, tricolor (dip, sage green and dark blue), *"Sacrifice Figure,"* mark: WEDGWOOD, ca. 1800, 2.5" x 2". *Courtesy of Dr. and Mrs. Victor Polikoff.* $1200-1500.

Perfume Bottle, light sage green (dip), *"Venus and Cupid,"* mark: none visible, early 19th century, 4.375" h. *Courtesy of Skinner, Inc., Boston and Bolton, Ma.* $500-700.

Perfume Bottle, tricolor (solid, light blue and sage green with silver lid), *"Venus and Cupid,"* mark: none visible, early 19th century, 3" h. *Courtesy of Skinner, Inc., Boston and Bolton, Ma.* $1500-1800.

Perfume Bottle, black (dip, brass base), *"Sacrifice Figures,"* mark: none visible, early 19th century, 3.75" h. *Courtesy of Skinner, Inc., Boston and Bolton, Ma.* $900-1100.

Perfume Bottle, tricolor (solid, pale blue and lilac with silver lid), *"Cybele,"* mark: none visible, early 19th century, 3.375" h. *Courtesy of Skinner, Inc., Boston and Bolton, Ma.* $1500-1800.

Perfume Bottle, dark blue (dip) with silver plated cover, *"Muses Watering Pegasus,"* mark: WEDGWOOD, ca. 1880, 2.75" x 2". *Author's Collection.* $600-800.

Perfume Bottle, dark blue (dip), *"Ganymede and the Eagle,"* mark: WEDGWOOD, ca. 1890, 2" x 2.25". *Author's Collection.* $300-400.

Perfume Bottle, dark blue (dip) with silver cover, *"Cybele,"* mark: WEDGWOOD, early 20th century, 3.5" h. *Courtesy of Skinner, Inc., Boston and Bolton, Ma.* $1400-1600.

Perfume Atomizer, dark blue (dip), *"Aurora,"* mark: WEDGWOOD, late 19th century, 2.625" h. *Courtesy of Skinner, Inc., Boston and Bolton, Ma.* $500-700.

Perfume Bottle, sage green (dip), *"Sacrifice Figures,"* mark: WEDGWOOD, MADE IN ENGLAND, ca. 1925, 4.75" x 2.5". *Anonymous Private Collection.* $400-500.

p. Plant Holders

Here we have another very broad category that covers a diverse range of Wedgwood Jasper items including, among other types, bough pots, bulb pots, flower pots, jardinières, pastille burners, and potpourris. This large group covers all periods from the eighteenth to the late twentieth century and, once again, runs the whole gamut from the mundane item one can hang or place on a porch to those that are usually seen only in museum collections. The photos in this section have been arranged alphabetically by type and then further arranged chronologically. Not included here are vases that have been fitted with potpourri or pierced lids. They will be found in the section devoted to vases.

Pair of Bough Pots, pale blue and white (solid), *"Zephyr and Flora,"* mark: WEDGWOOD, ca. 1790, 6" x 8". *Anonymous Private Collection.* $9000-11,000.

Pair of Cupid and Psyche Bough Pots, tricolor (solid, white, lilac and sage green), mark: WEDGWOOD, ca. 1790, 8.75" x 5". *Courtesy of the Buten Collection of Wedgwood at the Sands Point Preserve, Sands Point, N.Y.* $5000-6000.

Altars of Sacrifice (Incense Burners), pale blue (solid), mark: WEDGWOOD, 18th century, 4.75" h. *Courtesy of Skinner, Inc., Boston and Bolton, Ma.* $2500-3500.

Bough Pot, pale blue (solid), *"Classical Figure,"* mark: WEDGWOOD, 18th century, 9.25" h. *Courtesy of Skinner, Inc., Boston and Bolton, Ma.* $1000-1200.

Altar of Sacrifice (Incense Burner), diceware (dip, lilac with green quatrefoils), mark: WEDGWOOD, eighteenth century, 5.25" h. *Courtesy of Skinner, Inc., Boston and Bolton, Ma.* $8000-10,000.

Bough Pot (lid missing), pale blue (solid), *"Marine Venus,"* mark: WEDGWOOD, 18th century, 5.675" h. *Courtesy of Skinner, Inc., Boston and Bolton, Ma.* $800-1000.

Bough Pot, pale blue (solid), *"Cupid as Spring,"* mark: WEDGWOOD, 18th century, 7.75" h. *Courtesy of Skinner, Inc., Boston and Bolton, Ma.* $2000-3000.

Bough Pot, black (dip), *"Hope and the Anchor"* and *"Venus and Cupid,"* mark: WEDGWOOD, ca. 1800, 6" h.. *Courtesy of Skinner, Inc., Boston and Bolton, Ma.* $1200-1500.

Bough Pot, pale blue (solid), mark: WEDGWOOD, early 19th century, 7.125" h. ". *Courtesy of Skinner, Inc., Boston and Bolton, Ma.* $1500-1800.

Pair of Bulb Pots, lilac (solid), *"Four Seasons,"* mark: WEDGWOOD, ca. 1790, 6.25" x 5". *Courtesy of the Buten Collection of Wedgwood at the Sands Point Preserve, Sands Point, N.Y.* $5000-6000.

Bough Pot, pale blue (solid), *"Dancing Hours,"* mark: WEDGWOOD, 19th century, 5.5" h.. *Courtesy of Skinner, Inc., Boston and Bolton, Ma.* $1200-1500.

Bulb Pot, tricolor (dip, dark blue on pale blue), *"Apollo and Muses,"* mark: WEDGWOOD, ca. 1800, 5.5" x 8.5". ". *Courtesy of the Donald and Marsha Levine Ceramics and Glass Collection at the Sands Point Preserve, Sands Point, N.Y.* $2000-3000.

Pair of Bulb Pots, dark blue (dip) on pale blue ground, *"Muses,"* mark: WEDGWOOD, ca. 1790. *Anonymous Private Collection.* $1800-2000.

Bulb Pot, sage green (dip), *"Muses,"* mark: WEDGWOOD, ca. 1840, 5" x 8.25". *Courtesy of the Buten Collection of Wedgwood at the Sands Point Preserve, Sands Point, N.Y.* $2000-3000.

Component parts of above Bulb Pot.

Centerpiece, lilac (dip, supported by a Parian body in the form of a faun and a nymph), mark: WEDGWOOD, ca. 1866, 17.75" x 17". ". *Courtesy of the Donald and Marsha Levine Ceramics and Glass Collection at the Sands Point Preserve, Sands Point, N.Y.* $5000-7000.

Centerpiece (footed bowl and with stand), yellow buff and black (dip), mark: WEDGWOOD, ca. 1930, 5.5" x 9.75". *Courtesy of the Donald and Marsha Levine Ceramics and Glass Collection at the Sands Point Preserve, Sands Point, N.Y.* $3000-5000.

Fern Dish with stoneware lining, sage green (dip), "Sportive Love," mark: WEDGWOOD, ENGLAND, ca. 1900, 6" x 4". *Courtesy of Julie and Lance Pearce..* $400-500.

Flower Pot, diceware (dip, blue with sage green quatrefoils), mark: WEDGWOOD, ca. 1790, 4.75 x 5". *Courtesy of the Buten Collection of Wedgwood at the Sands Point Preserve, Sands Point, N.Y.* $2000-3000.

Flower Pot (Hedgehog) with Base, terra cotta (solid), mark: WEDGWOOD, MADE IN ENGLAND, 1971, 7" x 11". *Anonymous Private Collection.* $500-600.

Flower Pot with Pierced Cover, pale blue (dip), *"Sacrifice to Hymen,"* mark: WEDGWOOD, ca. 1800, 8.5" w. *Courtesy of Skinner, Inc., Boston and Bolton, Ma.* $2000-3000.

Flower Pot, dark blue (dip), mark: WEDGWOOD, ca. 1860, 2.5" x 5.25". *Anonymous Private Collection.* $800-1000.

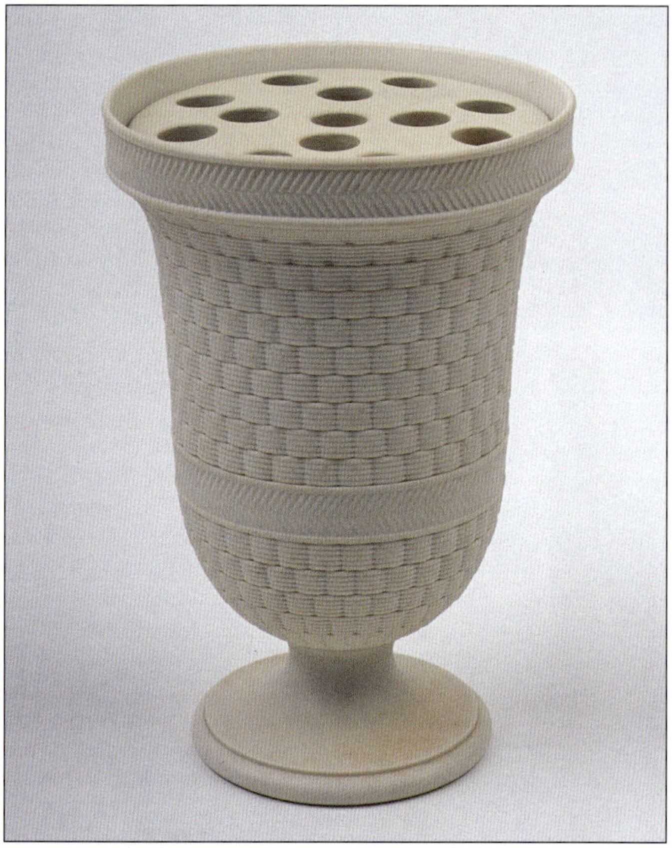

Flower Vase with Frog, white (solid), mark: WEDGWOOD, ca. 1880, 5.25" x 3.75". *Courtesy of Dr. and Mrs. Victor Polikoff.* $500-700.

Pair of Jardinières (Torches), black (dip), mark: WEDGWOOD, early 19th century, 4.75" h. *Courtesy of Skinner, Inc., Boston and Bolton, Ma.* $900-1100.

Hanging Planter, dark blue (dip), *"Sacrifice Figures,"* mark: WEDGWOOD, late 19th century, 6" h. *Courtesy of Skinner, Inc., Boston and Bolton, Ma.* $600-800.

Jardinière, lilac and white (dip), mark: WEDGWOOD, ca. 1810, 4.25" x 6.25". *Courtesy of Ellen Rubell.* $1000-1200.

Jardinière and Base, pale blue (solid), mark: WEDGWOOD, 18th century, 3.375" h. *Courtesy of Skinner, Inc., Boston and Bolton, Ma.* $1200-1500.

Louis XV Jardinière, tricolor (dip, pale blue and lilac), *"Henrietta Finch."* Mark: WEDGWOOD, ca. 1830. 6.5" x 10". *Courtesy of Adele Ierubino Barnett.* $1500-2000.

Pair of Miniature Jardinières on Stands, dark blue (dip), *"Three Graces" and "Cupid Market,"* mark: WEDGWOOD, ca. 1890, 2.5" h. *Courtesy of Skinner, Inc., Boston and Bolton, Ma.* $700-900.

Jardinière (317), tricolor (solid, white with sage green and lilac relief), mark: WEDGWOOD, late 19th century, 5.25"h. *Courtesy of Skinner, Inc., Boston and Bolton, Ma.* $1200-1500.

Jardinière, dark blue (dip), mark: WEDGWOOD + mustache marks, ca. 1840, 4.5" x 5". *Courtesy of Adele Ierubino Barnett.* $500-600.

Louis XV Jardinière, tricolor (dip, sage green and lilac), *"Henrietta Finch."* Mark: WEDGWOOD, ca. 1830. 6.75" x 9.5". *Anonymous Private Collection.* $1500-2000.

Jardinière (317), dark blue (dip), mark: WEDGWOOD, late 19th century, 6.75" h. *Courtesy of Skinner, Inc., Boston and Bolton, Ma.* $600-800.

Pastille Burner (Dolphin), dark blue (dip), mark: WEDGWOOD, ca. 1820, 4.5" x 5.25". *Courtesy of Dr. and Mrs. Victor Polikoff.* $3000-4000.

Pastille Burner, white and dark blue (solid), *"Cupid Asleep,"* mark: WEDGWOOD, ca. 1820, 7.75" h. *Courtesy of Skinner, Inc., Boston and Bolton, Ma.* $1000-1200.

Pastille Burner, tricolor (solid, black and yellow), mark: WEDGWOOD, Made in England, 1795 – 1995, 6" x 4.25. *Anonymous Private Collection.* $1000-1200.

Potpourri, pale blue (solid), mark: WEDGWOOD, 19th century, 2.5" h. *Courtesy of Skinner, Inc., Boston and Bolton, Ma.* $1000-1200.

Potpourri, dark blue (dip), *"Nike and the Warrior,"* mark: WEDGWOOD, 19th century, 2.75" h. *Courtesy of Skinner, Inc., Boston and Bolton, Ma.* $900-1100.

Potpourri (1000), dark blue (dip), mark: WEDGWOOD, ca. 1860, 7" x 7". *Courtesy of the Kerner Collection.* $1500-1800.

Pair of Potpourris (Footed), dark blue (dip), *"Classical Figures,"* mark: WEDGWOOD, late 19th century, 4.375" h. *Courtesy of Skinner, Inc., Boston and Bolton, Ma.* $1000-1200.

Pair of Potpourris, pale blue (solid), mark: WEDGWOOD, ca. 1860, 8.25" x 4.5". *Courtesy of the Donald and Marsha Levine Ceramics and Glass Collection at the Sands Point Preserve, Sands Point, N.Y.* $3000-5000.

Potpourri, dark blue (dip), *"Sacrifice Figures,"* mark: WEDGWOOD, ca. 1890, 4" x 6". *Author's Collection.* $350-450.

Potpourri (Frogmore), crimson (dip), *"Cupids at Play,"* mark: WEDGWOOD, ENGLAND, ca. 1925, 3" x 5". *Courtesy of Dr. and Mrs. Victor Polikoff.* $1500-1800.

q. Plaques

Plaques or tablets were originally intended as decorations for furniture, chimney pieces, and other domestic locations. To some extent they still serve this purpose, as they now adorn the walls of some of the finest Wedgwood collections. They have been manufactured since the eighteenth century in a variety of shapes, colors, and styles, and they are still produced in limited quantities in the modern era either as reproductions of earlier classics or as commemorative pieces to mark such events as the Olympics. In a certain sense plaques can be considered as larger versions of medallions and at times the division is not exactly clearly evident. The emphasis here is on classical subjects, including a number of representative pieces from the Wedgwood and Bentley as well as the Bert Bentley eras. For the purpose of organization, the photos have been divided into two basic geometric types and then listed chronologically.

Oval and Round Plaques

Included here are some examples of self-framed plaques where a second Jasper color is applied to a raised frame. Some of the mythological subjects used here, such as Medusa or the two concerning Diomedes and the Palladium, are among the most famous creations of the early Wedgwood period.

Plaque, pale blue (solid, in frame), *"Diomedes and the Paladium,"* mark: WEDGWOOD & BENTLEY, ca. 1775, 3" x 2.5. *Courtesy of Drs. Elaine and Jeffrey Tulman.* $4000-5000.

Plaque, bright blue (solid), *"Diomedes Gazing at the Palladium,"* mark: Wedgwood & Bentley, ca. 1776, 7.5" x 6". *Courtesy of the Buten Collection of Wedgwood at the Sands Point Preserve, Sands Point, N.Y.* $4000-5000.

Plaque, bright blue (solid, in metal mount), *"Urania,"* mark: WEDGWOOD & BENTLEY, ca. 1780. 7.5" x 5". *Courtesy of the Donald and Marsha Levine Ceramics and Glass Collection at the Sands Point Preserve, Sands Point, N.Y.* $2000-3000.

Plaque, bright blue (solid, in metal mount), *"Thalia,"* mark: WEDGWOOD & BENTLEY, ca. 1780. 7.5" x 5". *Courtesy of the Donald and Marsha Levine Ceramics and Glass Collection at the Sands Point Preserve, Sands Point, N.Y.* $2000-3000.

Plaque, white (solid), *"Thalia,"* mark: WEDGWOOD & BENTLEY, ca. 1775, 6" x 4 ".". *Courtesy of the Buten Collection of Wedgwood at the Sands Point Preserve, Sands Point, N.Y.* $2000-3000.

Plaque, white (solid), *"Melpomene,"* mark: WEDGWOOD & BENTLEY, ca. 1775, 6" x 4 ".". *Courtesy of the Buten Collection of Wedgwood at the Sands Point Preserve, Sands Point, N.Y.* $2000-3000.

Plaque, pale blue (solid), *"Herculaneum Figure,"* mark: WEDGWOOD & BENTLEY, ca. 1775, 10.25" x 7.25". *Anonymous Private Collection.* $20,000-25,000.

Plaque, bright blue (solid), *"Bacchanalian Figure,"* mark: WEDGWOOD & BENTLEY, ca. 1775, 6.5" x 4". *Courtesy of the Buten Collection of Wedgwood at the Sands Point Preserve, Sands Point, N.Y.* $2000-3000.

Plaque, pale blue (solid), *"Triumph of Bacchus,"* mark: WEDGWOOD & BENTLEY, ca. 1775, 7" x 10". *Courtesy of Jeffrey S. Milkins.* $7000-9000.

Plaque, pale blue (solid, in frame), *"Justice,"* mark: WEDGWOOD & BENTLEY, ca. 1775, 6.25" x 4.5". *Courtesy of Drs. Elaine and Jeffrey Tulman*. $1800-2000.

Plaque, pale blue (solid), *"Medusa,"* mark: WEDGWOOD & BENTLEY, ca. 1775, 5" diameter. *Courtesy of Drs. Elaine and Jeffrey Tulman*. $5000-7000.

Plaque, pale blue (solid, in frame), *"Minerva,"* mark: WEDGWOOD & BENTLEY, ca. 1775, 6.25" x 4.5". *Courtesy of Drs. Elaine and Jeffrey Tulman*. $1800-2000.

Plaque, black (dip), *"Infant Academy,"* mark: WEDGWOOD, ca. 1780, 5.75" x 6.5". *Courtesy of Edward L. Knowles*. $1800-2000.

Roundel (Circular Plaque), pale blue (solid), *"Centaur and Bacchante),"* mark: WEDGWOOD, ca. 1790, 15.5" diameter. *Courtesy of Drs. Elaine and Jeffrey Tulman.* $10,000-12,000.

Plaque in Frame, pale blue (solid), *"Venus Drawn by Swans,"* mark: WEDGWOOD, ca. 1790, 6" x 8.5" (including frame). *Anonymous Private Collection.* $1500-1800.

Plaque in Frame, pale blue (solid), *"Cupids Attending Swans,"* mark: WEDGWOOD, ca. 1790, 6" x 8.5" (including frame). *Anonymous Private Collection.* $1500-1800.

Plaque, pale blue (solid), *"Feast of the Gods,"* mark: WEDGWOOD, ca. 1790, 7" x 9.5". *Courtesy of Jeffrey S. Milkins.* $7000-9000.

Plaque, pale blue (solid), *"Minerva,"* mark: WEDGWOOD, ca. 1795, 4.25" x 3.25". *Courtesy of the Buten Collection of Wedgwood at the Sands Point Preserve, Sands Point, N.Y.* $1000-1200.

Plaque, dark blue (solid), *"Ganymede and the Eagle,"* mark: WEDGWOOD, ca. 1790, 6.5" x 4.75". *Courtesy of Jeffrey S. Milkins.* $2000-2500.

Plaque, light brown (dip), "Bacchanalian Figure," mark: WEDGWOOD, ca. 1800, 5" x 3.5". ". *Courtesy of the Buten Collection of Wedgwood at the Sands Point Preserve, Sands Point, N.Y.* $1000-1200.

Pair of Plaques, pale blue (solid), *"Cupid Stringing his Bow" and "Cupid Sharpening his Arrows,"* mark: WEDGWOOD, 19th century, 5" diameters. *Courtesy of Skinner, Inc., Boston and Bolton, Ma.* $1000-1200.

Pair of Plaques, sage green (dip), *"Ceres" and "Bacchanalian Figure,"* mark: WEDGWOOD, ca. 1890, 10" x 4.25". *Courtesy of Elizabeth and Paul Lauer.* $500-600 (each).

Plaque, sage green (dip), *"Melpomene,"* mark: WEDGWOOD, ca. 1880, 6.75" x 4.5". *Courtesy of Elizabeth and Paul Lauer.* $400-500.

Pair of Plaques, sage green (dip), *"Bacchanalian Figures,"* mark: WEDGWOOD, ca. 1890, 10" x 4.25". *Courtesy of Elizabeth and Paul Lauer.* $500-600 (each).

Self Framed Plaque, tricolor (pale blue and sage Green), "Mozart," mark: WEDGWOOD, ca. 1890, 3.5" x 2.25". *Courtesy of the Buten Collection of Wedgwood at the Sands Point Preserve, Sands Point, N.Y.* $600-700.

Plaque, pale blue (solid), *"Infant Academy,"* mark" WEDGWOOD, ca. 1790, 8.25" diameter. *Anonymous Private Collection.* $1000-1200.

Plaque, pale blue (dip), *"Perseus and Andromeda,"* mark: WEDGWOOD BB, ca. 1900 (modeled by Bert Bentley). 6.25" x 5.5". *Courtesy of Dr. and Mrs. Victor Polikoff.* $1200-1500.

Plaque, black (dip), *"Cleopatra,"* mark: WEDGWOOD, BB152 and oval "O" (modeled by Bert Bentley), ca. 1920, 6.75" diameter. *Courtesy of Jeffrey S. Milkins.* $2500-3000.

Pair of Self-Framed Plaques, tricolor (dip, pale and dark blue), *"Marriage of Cupid and Psyche" and "Sacrifice to Hymen,"* marks: WEDGWOOD, with oval 'O' & BB, ca. 1900 (modeled by Bert Bentley), 3.675" x 4.25". *Courtesy of Elizabeth and Paul Lauer.* $2000-3000 (for the pair).

Plaque, pale blue (dip) on white, *"Mercury,"* by Bert Bentley, mark WEDGWOOD, ca. 1935, 4" diameter. *Courtesy of Adele Ierubino Barnett.* $450-550.

Plaque, pale blue (solid), *"Dancing Lady,"* mark: WEDGWOOD, MADE IN ENGLAND, ca. 1960, 12" x 8". *Courtesy of Elizabeth and Paul Lauer.* $500-700.

Rectangular Plaques

Many of the friezes used on the rectangular Jasper plaques have been reproduced many times over the centuries, and some, such as the Dancing Hours, the Bacchanalian Triumph, and the series devoted to the Achilles story, are among the most recognizable of Wedgwood icons.

Plaque, sage green (dip), *"Vitruvian Scroll,"* mark: WEDGWOOD, eighteenth century, 7" x 18.25". *Courtesy of Skinner, Inc., Boston and Bolton, Ma.* $20,000-30,000.

Plaque, black (dip), *"Architectural Scroll,"* mark: WEDGWOOD, ca. 1790, 9" x 16". *Courtesy of Elizabeth and Paul Lauer.* $2500-3500.

Plaque, pale blue (solid), *"Bacchanalian Triumph,"* mark: WEDGWOOD, ca, 1800, 6" x 13.75". *Courtesy of Edward L. Knowles.* $1200-1500.

Plaque, sage green (dip), *"Priam Begging the Body of Hector from Achilles,"* mark: WEDGWOOD, ca. 1790, 5" x 10.5". *Courtesy of Edward L. Knowles.* $1500-1800.

Plaque, black (dip), *"Achilles Dragging Hector Around the Walls of Troy,"* mark: WEDGWOOD, ca. 1810, 20.5" x 7.75". *Courtesy of Edward L. Knowles.* $3000-5000.

Plaque, pale blue (dip), *"Diana Visiting Endymion,"* mark: WEDGWOOD, ca. 1820, 9.675" x 29.25". *Courtesy of Elizabeth and Paul Lauer.* $6000-8000.

Plaque, pale blue (dip), *"Birth and Dipping of Achilles,"* mark: WEDGWOOD, ca. 1840, 6" x 18.675". *Courtesy of Elizabeth and Paul Lauer.* $2000-3000.

Plaque, sage green (dip), *"Seven Ages of Man,"* mark: WEDGWOOD, ca. 1880 (modeled by Frederick Schenck), 10.25" x 25.5". *Courtesy of Elizabeth and Paul Lauer.* $5000-7000.

Plaque, pale blue (dip), *"Dancing Hours,"* mark: WEDGWOOD, ca. 1880, 6" x 18.25". *Courtesy of Elizabeth and Paul Lauer.* $2000-3000.

Plaque, sage green (dip), *"Sacrifice to Bacchus,"* mark: WEDGWOOD, ca. 1880, 8" x 18". *Courtesy of Elizabeth and Paul Lauer.* $3000-5000.

Plaque, tricolor (dip, sage green and pale blue), *"Trophy,"* mark: WEDGWOOD, mid-19th century, 17.75" x 5.5". *Courtesy of Skinner, Inc., Boston and Bolton, Ma.* $2500-3500.

Plaque, pale blue (dip), *"Diana,"* mark: WEDGWOOD, ca. 1880, 5.5" x 11.75". *Courtesy of Elizabeth and Paul Lauer.* $3000-4000.

Plaque, pale blue (solid), "The Canterbury Tales," mark: WEDGWOOD, ca. 1880 (modeled by Charles Toft), 6.5" x 13..75". *Courtesy of Elizabeth and Paul Lauer.* $1500-1800.

Plaque, tricolor (dip, sage green and yellow), *"Blind Man's Buff,"* mark: WEDGWOOD, ca. 1880, 6" x 18". *Courtesy of Edward L. Knowles.* $3500-4500.

Plaque, tricolor (dip, black and yellow), *"Dancing Hours,"* mark: WEDGWOOD, late 19th century, 6" x 13.75". *Courtesy of Skinner, Inc., Boston and Bolton, Ma.* $2000-3000.

Plaque, pale blue (solid), *"Minerva,"* mark: WEDGWOOD, ca. 1880, 11.675" x 7.25". *Courtesy of Elizabeth and Paul Lauer.* $4000-6000.

Plaque, tricolor (dip, pale blue and sage green), *"Blind Man's Buff,"* mark: WEDGWOOD, ca. 1890, 6" x 18.5". *Courtesy of Elizabeth and Paul Lauer.* $2500-3500.

Plaque, tricolor (dip, pale blue and sage green), *"Apollo and Muses,"* mark: WEDGWOOD, ca. 1890, 3.75" x 11". *Courtesy of Elizabeth and Paul Lauer.* $1500-2500.

Plaque, tricolor (dip, lilac and sage green), *"A Sacrifice,"* mark: WEDGWOOD, ca. 1890, 4.375" x 10.125". *Courtesy of Elizabeth and Paul Lauer.* $2000-3000.

Plaque, white (solid) with lilac relief, *"Muses,"* mark: WEDGWOOD, ca. 1890, 9" x 3.5". *Courtesy of Dr. and Mrs. Victor Polikoff.* $2000-3000.

Plaque, tricolor (dip, sage green and lilac), *" Blind Man's Buff,"* mark: WEDGWOOD, ENGLAND, ca. 1900, 5.5" x 11.25". *Courtesy of Edward L. Knowles.* $3500-4500.

Plaque, black (dip), *"Portland Vase Frieze,"* mark: WEDGWOOD, ENGLAND with oval "O", ca. 1900 (modeled by Bert Bentley), 8.5" x 22.25". *Courtesy of Elizabeth and Paul Lauer.* $4000-6000.

Plaque, pale blue (dip), *"Triumph of Bacchus and Ariadne,"* mark: WEDGWOOD with oval 'O' & BB, ca. 1900 (modeled by Bert Bentley), 10.5" x 27.25". *Courtesy of Elizabeth and Paul Lauer.* $10,000-12,000.

Plaque, sage green (solid), *"Hercules in the Garden of the Hesperides,"* mark: WEDGWOOD, MADE IN ENGLAND, 1968, 6" x 15.75". *Courtesy of Elizabeth and Paul Lauer.* $1500-2500.

Set of Four Plaques, pale blue (solid), *"Four Seasons,"* mark: WEDGWOOD and oval "O", ca. 1925 (modeled by Bert Bentley), 4" x 11.25". . *Courtesy of Skinner, Inc., Boston and Bolton, Ma.* $3500-4500.

Plaque, pale blue (solid), *"Fall of Phaeton,"* mark: WEDGWOOD, MADE IN ENGLAND, 1977 (originally modeled by George Stubbs in 18th century), 11.75" x 19.375. *Courtesy of Elizabeth and Paul Lauer.* $1500-2500.

Plaque, black (solid, with terracotta relief), *"Beloved of the Great Enchantress,"* mark: WEDGWOOD, MADE IN ENGLAND, 1979, 8.375" x 9". *Courtesy of Elizabeth and Paul Lauer.* $500-700.

Trophy Plate, diceware (dip, sage green with yellow quatrefoils), *"Zephyrs,"* mark: WEDGWOOD, ca. 1880, 8.75" diameter. *Courtesy of Dr. and Mrs. Victor Polikoff.* $3000-5000.

v. Plates and Trays

Plates and trays made of Wedgwood Jasper for both decorative and useful purposes have a history dating back to Josiah Wedgwood's time. From sparsely decorated little pin trays to wonderfully intricate Trophy plates, these items are easily mounted on walls and are thus highly collectible. While plates are almost uniformly round, trays can found in a variety of shapes. The small, modern, basically circular trays, usually designated as pin or ashtrays, are perhaps the most varied and popular Wedgwood Jasper collectible category. Both plates and trays have been utilized quite regularly for commemorative purposes.

Trophy Plate, white (solid, with sage green and lilac relief), *"Dipping of Achilles,"* mark: WEDGWOOD, ca. 1870, 8..75" diameter. *Courtesy of Jeffrey S. Milkins.* $2000-3000.

Trophy Plate, tricolor (dip, dark blue and lilac), *"Aurora,"* mark: WEDGWOOD, ca. 1880, 8.5" diameter. *Courtesy of the Kerner Collection.* $1500-1800.

Plate, black (dip), *"Zephyrs,"* mark: WEDGWOOD, 19th century, 9.125" diameter. *Courtesy of Skinner, Inc., Boston and Bolton, Ma.* $1000-1200.

Plate, sage green (dip), *"Zephyrs,"* mark: WEDGWOOD, ENGLAND, ca. 1900, 10" diameter. *Courtesy of the Kerner Collection.* $800-1000.

Plate, pale blue (dip), "Venus and Cupid," mark: WEDGWOOD, WUP = 1861 or 1887, 8.75" diameter. *Courtesy of Adele Ierubino Barnett.* $500-600.

Egyptian Plate, primrose (solid) with terracotta relief, *"Queen Ankhesenamum,"* limited edition, mark: WEDGWOOD, MADE IN ENGLAND, 1978, 8.5" diameter. *Courtesy of David Kroun.* $500-600.

Egyptian Plate, black (solid) with terracotta relief, "Tutankhamen," limited edition, mark: WEDGWOOD, MADE IN ENGLAND, 1978, 8.5" diameter. *Courtesy of David Kroun.* $500-600.

Platter, diceware (dip, dark blue with yellow quatrefoils), mark: WEDGWOOD, ca. 1795, 10.25" diameter. *Anonymous Private Collection.* $3000-4000.

Tray, sage green (dip), mark: WEDGWOOD, early 19th century, 15.625" diameter. *Courtesy of Skinner, Inc., Boston and Bolton, Ma.* $800-1000.

Comb Tray, dark blue (dip), *"Muses Watering Pegasus," "Aurora," etc.*, mark: WEDGWOOD, ca. 1890, 6.5" x 9.5". *Courtesy of the Buten Collection of Wedgwood at the Sands Point Preserve, Sands Point, N.Y.* $600-700.

Comb Tray, dark blue (dip), "Infant Academy," mark: WEDGWOOD, ENGLAND, ca. 1900, 11" x 8". *Courtesy of Adele Ierubino Barnett.* $600-700.

Roll Tray, dark blue (dip), "Caperns Birds," mark WEDGWOOD, MADE IN ENGLAND and CAPERNS, LTD., BRISTOL, 1934, 11" X 7.5". *Courtesy of Adele Ierubino Barnett.* $400-500.

Pin Tray (Octagon), dark blue (dip), *"Cupids at Play,"* mark: WEDGWOOD, ca. 1890, 3.25" x 4.5". *Author's Collection.* $200-300.

Pen Tray, wine (solid), mark: WEDGWOOD, MADE IN ENGLAND, 2002, 5.5" x 7.5. *Courtesy of David Kroun.* $250-350.

Tray, bright yellow (solid), mark: WEDGWOOD, MADE IN ENGLAND, ca. 2003, 4.25" diameter. *Courtesy of David Kroun.* $100-150.

s. Spill Vases

Spill vases had a very specific function. They were used to hold a small roll or twist of paper or slip of wood for lighting a fire. While most often made in a cylindrical shape (especially into the twentieth century), they came in a variety of shapes and styles and, judging by the vast amount of the more common varieties that have survived, they must have been very common household items. Shown here, however, is a group of the less common and more decorous types of spill vases, many of which were made with an engine turning lathe. Spill vases have been made since the invention of Jasper in 1775 and models were still being made in recent years.

Spill Vase (Corinthian), white (solid, sage green and lilac relief with engine turning), mark: WEDGWOOD, ca. 1875, 5.5" x 2.5". *Anonymous Private Collection.* $1500-1800.

Spill Vase (Corinthian), black (dip) with engine turning, mark: WEDGWOOD, ca. 1880, 3" x 2.25". *Anonymous Private Collection.* $800-1000.

Spill Vase (Corinthian), tricolor (dip, pale blue and lilac with engine turning), *"Cupid,"* mark: WEDGWOOD, mid-19th century, 3" h. *Courtesy of Skinner, Inc., Boston and Bolton, Ma.* $1000-1200.

Spill Vase, yellow (dip, with pale blue relief), mark: WEDGWOOD, 1814, 3.5" x 1.75". *Courtesy of Jeffrey S. Milkins.* $1500-1800.

Spill Vase (Cameo), tricolor (dip, sage green and lilac), mark: WEDGWOOD, 19th century, 3" h. *Courtesy of Skinner, Inc., Boston and Bolton, Ma.* $600-800.

Spill Vase (Upright), tricolor (dip, yellow with pale blue relief), mark: WEDGWOOD, mid-19th century, 3.875" h. *Courtesy of Skinner, Inc., Boston and Bolton, Ma.* $1000-1200.

Spill Vase (Cameo), tricolor (dip, pale blue and sage green), *"Classical Figures,"* mark: WEDGWOOD, mid-19th century, 3" h. *Courtesy of Skinner, Inc., Boston and Bolton, Ma.* $700-900.

Spill Vase, black (dip, with engine turning), mark: WEDGWOOD, ca. 1820, 3.25" h. *Courtesy of Skinner, Inc., Boston and Bolton, Ma.* $700-900.

Spill Vase (Cameo), tricolor (dip, dark blue and lilac), mark: WEDGWOOD, mid-19th century, 3" h. *Courtesy of Skinner, Inc., Boston and Bolton, Ma.* $700-900.

Spill Vase (Upright), sage green (dip, with engine turning), *"Dancing Hours,"* mark: WEDGWOOD, early 19th century, 5.375" h. *Courtesy of Skinner, Inc., Boston and Bolton, Ma.* $700-900.

Spill Vase, lilac (dip with engine turning), mark: WEDGWOOD, ca. 1870, 4" x 2.5". *Courtesy of the Donald and Marsha Levine Ceramics and Glass Collection at the Sands Point Preserve, Sands Point, N.Y.* $600-700.

Spill Vase (Upright), dark blue (dip), sgraffito trial piece signed by Harry Barnard, mark: WEDGWOOD, ENGLAND, 1898, 2.75" x 1.25. *Courtesy of the Buten Collection of Wedgwood at the Sands Point Preserve, Sands Point, N.Y.* $1500-2000.

Spill Vase, pale blue (dip with engine turning), mark: WEDGWOOD®, MADE IN ENGLAND, 1997, 6.25" x 3". *Courtesy of Adele Ierubino Barnett.* $650-750.

t. Tea and Coffee Sets, etc.

The second half of the eighteenth century saw the burgeoning of tea and coffee consumption in Great Britain. The pots needed to brew these products were being imported from China when the Staffordshire potters saw a golden opportunity to expand into a new market. Wedgwood, naturally, was in the forefront of this development and, at a very early stage, started producing tea and coffee pots as well as the other items that accompanied them. As can be seen here, wonderful examples of tea pots, coffee pots, sugar bowls, and creamers have been consistently designed and produced in Jasper over the last two and a half centuries. They were often sold together with matching trays and cups and saucers as dejeuner sets.

Pair of Coffee Pots, bright blue (solid) and sage green (solid with engine turning), *"Domestic Employment,"* marks: WEDGWOOD, ca. 1790, 8.5" x 6" and 9" x 6.5". *Anonymous Private Collection.* $900-1100 (blue), $1200-1500 (green).

Dejeuner Set, pale blue (solid), mark: WEDGWOOD, ca. 1790, 15.5" (tray). *Courtesy of Elizabeth and Paul Lauer.* $4000-6000.

Teapot, lilac (dip), mark: WEDGWOOD, 18th century, 5.5" h. *Courtesy of Skinner, Inc., Boston and Bolton, Ma.* $1000-1200.

Five Piece Partial Tea Set, sage green (dip), marks: WEDGWOOD, 18th century, 4" h. (teapot), 2.75" h. (creamer), 4.25" h. (sugar), 5.5" h. (hot water pot), 4.625" diameter (saucer). *Courtesy of Skinner, Inc., Boston and Bolton, Ma.* $2500-3500.

Teapot, pale blue (solid), *"Boys at Play,"* mark: WEDGWOOD, 18th century, 5.125" h. *Courtesy of Skinner, Inc., Boston and Bolton, Ma.* $1000-1200.

Teapot, sage green (dip, with engine turning), *"Boys at Play,"* mark: WEDGWOOD, ca. 1790, 4" x 6.5". *Courtesy of Drs. Elaine and Jeffrey Tulman*. $3000-4000.

Teapot, pale blue (dip, with engine turning), *"Domestic Employment,"* WEDGWOOD, ca. 1790, 4" x 6.5". *Courtesy of the Kerner Collection.* $1800-2000.

Teapot, pale blue (solid), *"Boys at Play,"* mark: WEDGWOOD, ca. 1790, 6" x 6.5". *Courtesy of Jeffrey S. Milkins.* $2000-3000.

Teapot, lilac (dip, with engine turning), *"Boys at Play,"* mark: WEDGWOOD, ca. 1790, 4.5" x 5". *Courtesy of Ellen Rubell.* $1500-1700.

Teapot, pale blue (solid), *"Virgo,"* mark: WEDGWOOD, ca. 1785, 4.25" x 5 .75" *Courtesy of Edward L. Knowles.* $1000-1200.

Sugar Bowl, diceware (dip, lilac with green quatrefoils), mark: WEDGWOOD, ca. 1790, 4" x 3.25". *Courtesy of Drs. Elaine and Jeffrey Tulman.* $3000-4000.

Teapot (Footed), pale blue (solid), *"Domestic Employment,"* mark: WEDGWOOD, c. 1790, 7" x 8". *Anonymous Private Collection.* $7000-9000.

Creamer, diceware (dip, sage green with yellow quatrefoils), mark: WEDGWOOD, ca. 1800, 2.5" x 3". *Courtesy of Drs. Elaine and Jeffrey Tulman.* $1800-2000.

Coffee Set , pale blue (solid), *"Cupids,"* marks: WEDGWOOD, early 19th century, 8.325" h. (coffee pot), 5.625 h. (sugar), 6" h. (creamer). *Courtesy of Skinner, Inc., Boston and Bolton, Ma.* $1200-1500.

Teapot, four color diceware (dip, dark blue with sage green quatrefoils and pale blue spout), mark: WEDGWOOD, ca. 1800, 3.5" h. *Courtesy of Skinner, Inc., Boston and Bolton, Ma.* $2000-3000.

Teapot, sage green (dip), *"Boys at Play,"* mark: WEDGWOOD, ca. 1840. 4.125" h. *Courtesy of Skinner, Inc., Boston and Bolton, Ma.* $1200-1500.

Tea Pot (Octagon), dark blue (dip), *"Two Graces,"* mark: WEDGWOOD, early 19th century, 5.125" h. *Courtesy of Skinner, Inc., Boston and Bolton, Ma.* $600-800.

Creamer, dark blue (dip) with star and fern pattern, mark: WEDGWOOD, ca. 1840, 3" x 6". *Courtesy of the Buten Collection of Wedgwood at the Sands Point Preserve, Sands Point, N.Y.* \$600-800

Teapot, diceware (dip, black with yellow quatrefoils), mark: WEDGWOOD, early 19th century, 4.25" h. *Courtesy of Skinner, Inc., Boston and Bolton, Ma.* \$3000-5000.

Sugar Box, tricolor (dip, sage green and lilac), mark: WEDGWOOD, early 19th century, 3.75" x 3.25". *Courtesy of Stamford Auction, Stamford, Ct.* \$800-1000.

Six Piece Tea Set (Trophy), tricolor (dip, sage green and lilac), marks: WEDGWOOD, mid-19th century, 3.675" h. (teapot , sugar and creamer), 5" diameter (bowl). *Courtesy of Skinner, Inc., Boston and Bolton, Ma.* \$5000-7000.

Coffee Set, pale blue (dip, with engine turning and silver plated mounts), marks: WEDGWOOD, late 19th century, 5.875" h (coffee pot). *Courtesy of Skinner, Inc., Boston and Bolton, Ma.* \$1800-2000.

Teapot, black (dip), *"Aurora,"* mark: WEDGWOOD, late 19th century, 4.5" h. *Courtesy of Skinner, Inc., Boston and Bolton, Ma.* $900-1100.

Tea Set (St. Louis), tricolor (solid, white with sage green and lilac relief), mark: WEDGWOOD, marks: WEDGWOOD, ca. 1880, 3.5" h. (teapot), *Courtesy of Skinner, Inc., Boston and Bolton, Ma.* $1500-1800.

Teapot, diceware (solid, pale blue with sage green quatrefoils), mark: WEDGWOOD, 19th century, 3.625" h. *Courtesy of Skinner, Inc., Boston and Bolton, Ma.* $1200-1500.

Tea Set, diceware (dip, sage green with yellow quatrefoils), mark: WEDGWOOD, ca. 1900, 4" h. (teapot). *Courtesy of Skinner, Inc., Boston and Bolton, Ma.* $3000-5000.

Miniature Coffee Pot, lilac (dip), "Coriolanus," mark: WEDGWOOD, ENGLAND, ca. 1900, 2.625" h. *Courtesy of Skinner, Inc., Boston and Bolton, Ma.* $800-1000.

Creamer, sage green (dip), *"Friendship Consoling Affliction,"* mark: WEDGWOOD, ENGLAND, ca. 1900, 2" x 4". *Courtesy of the Kerner Collection.* $300-400.

Sugar Bowl, olive green (dip), *"Sacrifice Figures,"* mark: WEDGWOOD, ENGLAND, ca. 1900, 3" x 5". *Courtesy of the Kerner Collection.* $300-500.

Biggin (shown on following page) with matching Sugar and Creamer, (dip, with brass mountings), *"Three Graces" and "Sacrifice Figures,"* mark: WEDGWOOD, England, ca. 1900, various sizes. *Courtesy of the Buten Collection of Wedgwood at the Sands Point Preserve, Sands Point, N.Y.* $2000-2500.

Biggin, sage green (dip, with brass mountings), *"Three Graces" and "Sacrifice Figures,"* mark: WEDGWOOD, England, ca. 1900, 7.5" x 5.5". *Courtesy of the Buten Collection of Wedgwood at the Sands Point Preserve, Sands Point, N.Y.* $1000-1200.

Component parts of previous item

Tea Set (146), yellow buff (dip, with black relief), *"Sacrifice Figures," etc.,* marks: WEDGWOOD, MADE IN ENGLAND, ca. 1930, 4" x 7" (teapot), *Courtesy of Elizabeth and Paul Lauer.* $2000-3000.

Coffee Set, black (dip, black and primrose with black relief and engine turning), mark: WEDGWOOD, MADE IN ENGLAND, 1980, 8.25" h. (coffee pot), 4" h. (sugar), 3" h. (creamer). *Courtesy of Skinner, Inc., Boston and Bolton, Ma.* $1800-2000.

Coffee Pot, dark blue (dip, with spaniel finial), *"Muses,"* mark: WEDGWOOD, ca. 1930, 9.75" h. *Courtesy of Skinner, Inc., Boston and Bolton, Ma.* $1500-2500.

Teapot, black (solid, with tan relief), *"Dancing Hours,"* mark: WEDGWOOD, MADE IN ENGLAND, 2005, 3" x 5". *Courtesy of the Kerner Collection.* $150-250.

Tea Set (Octagon), tricolor (solid, pale blue and sage green), *"Hope and the Anchor,"* mark: WEDGWOOD, MADE IN ENGLAND, 2000 (limited edition of 100), 5" x 7.25" (teapot), *Courtesy of Elizabeth and Paul Lauer.* $1000-1200.

u. Tobacciana

Tobacco was brought to England in the sixteenth century by Sir Walter Raleigh and its consumption grew over the next two hundred years. In Josiah Wedgwood's time it was most often smoked in pipes or sniffed as snuff. Pipes in Jasper were first made during the Wedgwood and Bentley partnership and these and other tobacco related products have been steadily made ever since. These include tobacco jars (also known as humidors), snuffboxes, ashtrays, and pipe stands. While matchboxes have uses well beyond tobacco, they are included in this category as they are a closely related product. Items in this section are arranged alphabetically by type.

Ash Tray and Match Striker, sage green (dip, with silver plated mount), *"Horses"* (modeled by Edward Burch) mark: WEDG-WOOD, ca. 1920, 2" x 3.25". *Courtesy of the Buten Collection of Wedgwood at the Sands Point Preserve, Sands Point, N.Y.* $700-800.

Ash tray (heart), dark blue (dip), *"Wembley British Empire Exhibition Arms,"* mark: WEDGWOOD, MADE IN ENGLAND, 1924. 4.5" x 4.25". *Courtesy of Adele Ierubino Barnett.* $150-250.

Cigar Rest, tricolor (dip, yellow with pale blue relief), *"Cupid Disarmed," etc.* mark: WEDGWOOD, ca. 1868, 4" l. *Courtesy of Skinner, Inc., Boston and Bolton, Ma.* $700-900.

Match Box (cylinder), dark blue (dip, with no relief), mark: WEDGWOOD, ca. 1870, 1.75" x 1.75". *Courtesy of Adele Ierubino Barnett.* $300-400.

Cigarette Jar, tricolor (solid, pale blue with white and Portland blue relief), *"Offering to Peace,"* mark: WEDGWOOD, MADE IN ENGLAND, 1988, 4.5" x 3.5".
Courtesy of David Kroun. $200-300

Match Box (Berlin with Cover), sage green (dip), *"Sportive Love,"* mark: WEDGWOOD, 1879, 6" x 4". *Courtesy of Shapiro Auctions, Australia.* $800-1000.

Match Box (Taper), dark blue (dip), *"The Procession" and "Cupid as Oracle,"* mark: WEDGWOOD, ca. 1880, 3.5" x 2.5". *Author's Collection.* $500-600.

Match Box (Taper), *"Infant Jupiter Being Fed by a of the Daughter of Melisseus,"* mark: WEDGWOOD, ca. 1890, 3.5" x 2.5". *Author's Collection.* $500-600.

Match Box (Square), yellow (dip), *"Domestic Employment,"* mark: WEDGWOOD, ca. 1880, 3.75" x 2". *Courtesy of the Kerner Collection.* $700-900.

Match Box (Oval), tricolor (dip, yellow with pale blue relief), *"Bellerophon Watering Pegasus,"* mark: WEDGWOOD, ENGLAND, ca. 1900, 3.75" l. *Courtesy of Skinner, Inc., Boston and Bolton, Ma.* $700-900.

Match Box (Gein), chocolate brown (dip), *"Coriolanus,"* mark: WEDGWOOD, MADE IN ENGLAND, ca. 1910, 2.75" h. *Courtesy of Skinner, Inc., Boston and Bolton, Ma.* $700-900.

Matchbox Holder, yellow (dip), *"Nike and the Warrior,"* mark WEDGWOOD, ENGLAND, ca. 1900, 3.75" x 4.25". *Courtesy of Jeffrey S. Milkins.* $500-700.

Pipe Stem Stand, medium blue (dip), mark: WEDGWOOD, ca. 1890, 2.25" x 5". *Author's Collection.* $500-600.

Pipe Stand and Pipe Bowl, dark blue (dip), *"Muses Watering Bellerophon,"* mark: WEDGWOOD, ca. 1880, 5.75" x 4". *Anonymous Private Collection.* $900-1000.

Two Snuff Bottles, sage green and dark blue (dip), *"Royal Arms of the United Kingdom" and "Nike and the Warrior,"* marks: WEDGWOOD, ENGLAND, 2.5" x 2". *Courtesy of Dr. and Mrs. Victor Polikoff.* $250-350 (each).

Snuff Box, dark blue (dip, with screw-on lid), *"Psyche Bound to a Tree by Cupids,"* mark: WEDGWOOD, ca. 1880, 1" x 3.25". *Author's Collection.* $500-600.

Tobacco Jar (Taper), lilac (dip), *"Icarus and Daedelus,"* mark: WEDGWOOD, JBW = 1868, 6" x 4.25". *Courtesy of Ellen Rubell.* $700-900.

Open view of previous item

Bottom view of previous item

Tobacco Jar (Greek Key), dark blue (dip), *"Muses" and "Zephyrs,"* mark: WEDGWOOD, ca. 1880, 4" x 4". *Author's Collection.* $500-600.

Tobacco Jar (Acorn), lilac (dip), *"Boys at Play,"* mark: WEDGWOOD, YZK = 1882, 6.75" x 5". *Courtesy of Ellen Rubell.* $600-800.

Tobacco Jar, tricolor (solid, pale blue and lilac), *"Cupids,"* mark: WEDGWOOD, late 19th century, 4" x 4". *Courtesy of Skinner, Inc., Boston and Bolton, Ma.* $800-1000.

Tobacco Jar, pale blue (dip), *"Dancing Hours,"* mark: WEDGWOOD, ca. 1890, 6.5" x 4.75". *Courtesy of the Kerner Collection.* $500-700.

Tobacco Jar with Candle Holder, pale blue (dip), *"Smoking Motifs,"* mark: WEDGWOOD, ENGLAND, ca.1895, 5.625" h. *Courtesy of Skinner, Inc., Boston and Bolton, Ma.* $600-800.

Tobacco Jar (Upright with Harry Barnard motto design), dark blue (dip), Motto: "For Rich or Poor, in Peace or Strife, it Soothes the Rugged Path of Life," mark: WEDGWOOD, ENGLAND, ca. 1895, 5" x 4.5". *Courtesy of Adele Ierubino Barnett.* $600-700.

Tobacco Jar (Dome with Harry Barnard motto design), dark blue (dip), Motto: *"For Rich or Poor, in Peace or Strife, it Soothes the Rugged Path of Life"*, mark: WEDGWOOD, ENGLAND, ca. 1895, 7" h. *Courtesy of Skinner, Inc., Boston and Bolton, Ma.* $700-900.

Tobacco Jar with Candle Holder, dark blue (dip), *"Smoking Motifs,"* mark: WEDGWOOD, ENGLAND, ca.1895, 5.25" x 5". *Courtesy of Adele Ierubino Barnett.* $600-800.

Tobacco Jar, pale blue (solid), *"Pomona,"* mark: WEDGWOOD, MADE IN ENGLAND, 1985 (Limited Edition of 200 in the 'Wedgwood Masterpiece Collection'), 9" h. *Courtesy of Skinner, Inc., Boston and Bolton, Ma.* $800-1000.

Tobacco Jar (Laurel), dark blue (dip), *"Offering to Peace,"* mark: WEDGWOOD, ENGLAND, ca. 1900, 6.5" x 4.5". *Author's Collection.* $400-500.

Tobacco Jar, gray (solid), *"Sacrifice Figures,"* mark: WEDGWOOD, MADE IN ENGLAND, 1991, 6.25" x 4.5". *Courtesy of the Kerner Collection.* $250-350.

v. Vases

In terms of numbers, this is by far the largest category in the Gallery. It reflects the undeniable fact that, in the Company's long history, vases have always been the greatest outlet for creativity among the designers and potters that Wedgwood employed. Also reflected are the popularity of vases among collectors and the sheer abundance of wonderful specimens seen in all the collections that were visited for the purpose of writing this book. No distinction is made here between vases and urns as most Wedgwood references list all types as vases whether they have a cover or not. The vases range from the simplest bud vase to the most complex shapes imaginable and chronologically cover the productions of the previous quarter millennium. For the sake of manageability, the pages devoted to vases have been broken down into a number of distinct sections. The initial sections cover many of the most famous types of vases that have names. Next comes a large group whose names and/or shape numbers has been found by the author while the final group of vases lacks any specific identification.

Bamboo Vases

This type of vase which was obviously influenced by Chinese originals was first made in Jasper by Wedgwood around 1790. Some versions have two or three bamboo stems while others have four. Most examples of this classic Wedgwood vase are from earlier periods, but this shape was reproduced in 1977-8 as part of the Primrose Collection.

Vase (Bamboo - 542), black (dip), mark: WEDGWOOD, early 19th century, 10.5" h. *Courtesy of Skinner, Inc., Boston and Bolton, Ma.* $4000-6000.

Vase (Bamboo –542), pale blue (solid), mark: WEDGWOOD, ca. 1795, 8" x 4". *Courtesy of the Donald and Marsha Levine Ceramics and Glass Collection at the Sands Point Preserve, Sands Point, N.Y.* $2000-3000.

Barber Bottles

The name "barber bottle" has been given by collectors to a group of vase shapes that all have stoppers and have the appropriate form for such tonsorial purposes. The most ornate type, shape number 1110, has been made in many different Jasper colors including tricolor and four-color versions. The other vases in this group, while not as elaborately decorated and considerably more common, are still very attractive and highly collectible.

Pair of Vases (Barber Bottles – 1012), tricolor (solid, white with sage green and lilac relief), mark: WEDGWOOD, late 19th century, 5.75" h. *Courtesy of Skinner, Inc., Boston and Bolton, Ma.* $1200-1500.

Vase (Barber Bottle – 1014), sage green (dip). *"Polymnia and Thalia,"* mark: WEDGWOOD, ENGLAND, ca. 1900, 7.5" x 3.5". *Courtesy of the Buten Collection of Wedgwood at the Sands Point Preserve, Sands Point, N.Y.* $500-600.

Pair of Vases (Barber Bottles – 988), dark blue (dip), *"Cupid" and "Sacrifice to Peace,"* mark: WEDGWOOD, early 19th century, 7.25" h. . *Courtesy of Skinner, Inc., Boston and Bolton, Ma.* $1000-1200.

Pair of Vases (Barber Bottles – 1110), black (dip), *"Jupiter" and "Sacrifice to Peace,"* mark: WEDGWOOD, ca. 1860, 11.5" x 7.5". *Courtesy of Edward L. Knowles.* $3500-4500.

Vase (Barber Bottle -1110), tricolor (dip, lilac and sage green), *"Cybele,"* mark: WEDGWOOD, ca. 1880, 10.25" x 6.25". *Courtesy of Edward L. Knowles.* $2500-3500.

Pair of Vases (Barber Bottles – 1110), tricolor (solid, white with sage green and lilac relief), *"An Offering to Jupiter" and "Sportive Love,"* mark: WEDGWOOD, ca. 1870, 10.25" x 6.25". *Courtesy of Edward L. Knowles.* $4500-6500.

Vase (Barber Bottle -1110), four color (dip, sage green, dark blue and lilac), *"Muses Watering Pegasus,"* mark: WEDGWOOD, ca. 1880, 10.75" x 6.75". *Courtesy of Edward L. Knowles.* $3500-4500.

Vase (Barber Bottle – 1110), tricolor (dip, pale blue and lilac), *"Coriolanus,"* mark: WEDG-WOOD MGC = 1874, 10.5" x 5.5". *Courtesy of the Kerner Collection.* $1500-2500.

Pair of Vases (1110 – Barber Bottles), tricolor (dip, dark blue and lilac), *"Psyche Bound to a Tree by Cupids,"* mark: WEDGWOOD, ca. 1870, 11" x 7.5". *Courtesy of the Buten Collection of Wedgwood at the Sands Point Preserve, Sands Point, N.Y.* $2000-3000.

Mask detail on above Barber Bottles (1110)

Campana Vases

Named after a region in Southern Italy where many ancient prototypes had been unearthed, the Campana vases have inverted bell shapes usually with upturned handles. They have been consistently produced in Jasper since the eighteenth century and can be seen with or without handles or lids (which can be solid or pierced) or affixed atop plinths or drum bases.

Vase (Campana - 43) with Pierced Lid, dark blue (dip), *"Muses,"* mark: WEDGWOOD, ca. 1880, 15" x 9". *Courtesy of the Kerner Collection.* $2500-3500.

Vase (Campana – 43) with Pierced Lid, dark blue (dip), *"Bacchanalian Triumph,"* mark: WEDGWOOD, ca. 1810, 17.25" x 7". *Courtesy of Edward L. Knowles.* $4000-6000.

Vase (Campana – 43), dark blue (dip), mark: WEDGWOOD, ca. 1880, 10.25" h. *Courtesy of Skinner, Inc., Boston and Bolton, Ma.* $2500-3500.

Vase (Campana – 43), pale blue (dip), "Sacrifice Figures," mark: WEDGWOOD, ENGLAND, ca. 1900, 18" x 8". *Courtesy of Edward L. Knowles.* $3000-4000.

Vase (Campana), dark blue (dip), mark: WEDGWOOD, ca. 1860, 14" x 6.5". *Courtesy of the Buten Collection of Wedgwood at the Sands Point Preserve, Sands Point, N.Y.* $1200-1500.

Vase (Campana - 43), sage green (solid) with white and lilac relief, *"Offering to Peace,"* mark: WEDGWOOD, MADE IN ENGLAND, ca. 1980, 11.25" x 5.25". *Courtesy of the Buten Collection of Wedgwood at the Sands Point Preserve, Sands Point, N.Y.* $1200-1500.

Pair of Vases (Campana – 495) on Drum Bases, tricolor (solid, white with sage green and lilac relief), *"Hope and the Anchor," etc.*, mark: WEDGWOOD, mid-19th century, 6.25" h. *Courtesy of Skinner, Inc., Boston and Bolton, Ma.* $1500-1800.

Pair of Vases (Campana – 495) on Drum Bases, lilac (dip), *"Bacchanalian Boys,"* mark: WEDGWOOD, ca. 1867, 16" h. *Courtesy of Skinner, Inc., Boston and Bolton, Ma.* $8000-10,000.

Vase (Campana – 495 – missing cover), diceware (dip, sage green with yellow quatrefoils), mark: WEDGWOOD, late 19th century, 6,5" h. *Courtesy of Skinner, Inc., Boston and Bolton, Ma.* $1200-1500.

Vase (Campana with Borghese relief – 1185), pale blue (solid), *"Bacchanalian Triumph,"* mark: WEDGWOOD, ca. 1790, 19.5" h. *Courtesy of Skinner, Inc., Boston and Bolton, Ma.* $10,000-15,000.

Vase (Campana – 1153), lilac (dip), *"Muses,"* mark: WEDGWOOD, ca. 1870, 12.25" x 6.75". *Courtesy of Jeffrey S. Milkins.* $1800-2000.

Vase (681) with Pierced Lid on Drum Base, pale blue (dip), *"Sportive Love,"* mark: WEDGWOOD, ca. 1864, 6.625" h. ". *Courtesy of Skinner, Inc., Boston and Bolton, Ma.* $700-900.

Vase (Campana – 1153), tricolor (dip, pale blue and sage green), *"Muses,"* mark: WEDGWOOD, 19th century, 12.25" h. . *Courtesy of Skinner, Inc., Boston and Bolton, Ma.* $1500-1800.

Vase (Campana – 1153), tricolor (solid, white with sage green and lilac relief), *"Classical Figures,"* mark: WEDGWOOD, late 19th century, 12.5" h. *Courtesy of Skinner, Inc., Boston and Bolton, Ma.* $1000-1200.

Canopic Vases

Based on Ancient Egyptian funerary urns, these stunning two piece vases were produced in Jasper during the nineteenth century and reflected a fascination with all things Egyptian, spurred by the discovery and decipherment of the Rosetta Stone. The form was revived in 1978 with new color combinations for a new Egyptian craze caused by the worldwide traveling show of the treasures unearthed decades before from the tomb of Pharoah Tutankhamen.

Canopic Vase, dark blue and white (dip), mark: WEDGWOOD, early 19th century, 10" h. *Courtesy of Skinner, Inc., Boston and Bolton, Ma.* $5000-7000.

Canopic Vase, lilac and white (dip) and white, mark: WEDGWOOD, ca. 1870, 10" x 5". *Courtesy of Jeffrey S. Milkins.* $5000-7000.

Canopic Vase, pale blue and white (dip), mark: WEDGWOOD, ca. 1850, 9..75" x 5.25". ". *Courtesy of the Donald and Marsha Levine Ceramics and Glass Collection at the Sands Point Preserve, Sands Point, N.Y.* $4000-6000.

Canopic Vase, sage green and white (dip), mark: WEDGWOOD, WJW = 1868, 9.5" h. *Courtesy of Skinner, Inc., Boston and Bolton, Ma.* $-6000.

Canopic Vase, primrose (solid, with terracotta relief), mark: WEDGWOOD, MADE IN ENGLAND, 1978, 9.5" h. *Courtesy of Skinner, Inc., Boston and Bolton, Ma.* $1200-1500.

Dancing Hours Vases

As one of the most famous and popular of Wedgwood bas-relief subjects, it was only natural that the Dancing Hours would regularly be featured on several types of Jasper vases. Most frequently seen is the number 275 shape that has been produced almost without break since the early nineteenth century. It has been made in many different colors (including tricolor combinations) and has very prominent satyr mask handles. Other varieties of Dancing Hours vases have been made with diceware and other engine turned patterns.

Vase (275), lilac (dip), *"Dancing Hours,"* mark: WEDGWOOD, ca. 1870, 7.75" x 3.75". *Anonymous Private Collection.* $1000-1200.

Pair of Vases (275), pale sage green (dip), *"Dancing Hours,"* mark: WEDGWOOD, mid-19th century, 8.5" h. . *Courtesy of Skinner, Inc., Boston and Bolton, Ma.* $2000-3000.

Vase (275), tricolor (dip, yellowish green with yellow and white relief), *"Dancing Hours,"* mark: WEDGWOOD, ca. 1880, 9" x 4.75" *Courtesy of Edward L. Knowles.* $1800-2000.

Vase (275), tricolor (dip, dark blue and sage green), *"Dancing Hours,"* mark: WEDGWOOD, late 19th century, 9.75" h. *Courtesy of Skinner, Inc., Boston and Bolton, Ma.* $1200-1500.

Vase (275), tricolor ((solid, white with sage green wash in center plus lilac and sage green relief), *"Dancing Hours,"* mark: WEDGWOOD, ENGLAND, ca. 1895, 21.25" x 8.25". *Courtesy of Jeffrey S. Milkins.* $5000-7000.

Vase (275), dark blue (dip), *"Dancing Hours,"* mark: WEDGWOOD, ENGLAND, ca. 1900, 6.75" x 3.25". *Author's Collection.* $500-700.

Vase (275), yellow (dip), *"Dancing Hours,"* mark: WEDGWOOD, ENGLAND, ca. 1900, 6" x 3". *Courtesy of the Kerner Collection.* $1200-1500.

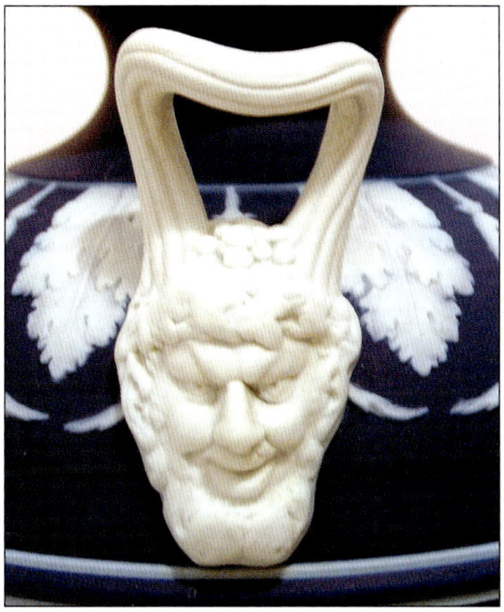

Mask handle detail on the 275 Dancing Hours vases.

Vase (275), lilac (solid), *"Dancing Hours,"* mark: WEDGWOOD, MADE IN ENGLAND, 1960, 11" x 5". *Anonymous Private Collection.* $500-600.

Vase (273), diceware (dip, pale blue with sage green quatrefoils), *"Dancing Hours,"* mark: WEDGWOOD, ca. 1800, 8.25" x 4". *Courtesy of the Buten Collection of Wedgwood at the Sands Point Preserve, Sands Point, N.Y.* $4000-5000.

Vase (273), diceware (dip, lilac with green quatrefoils), *"Dancing Hours,"* mark: WEDGWOOD, early 19th century, 8.5" h. *Courtesy of Skinner, Inc., Boston and Bolton, Ma.* $1200-1500.

Vase (273), pale blue (dip), *"Dancing Hours,"* mark: WEDGWOOD, ca. 1870, 16.5" x 5". *Courtesy of the Kerner Collection.* $1800-2000.

Vase (273), diceware (dip, black with yellow quatrefoils), *"Dancing Hours,"* mark: WEDGWOOD, mid-19th century, 8.75" h. *Courtesy of Skinner, Inc., Boston and Bolton, Ma.* $1500-1800.

Vase (1202), light blue (dip, with engine turning), mark: WEDGWOOD, ca. 1880, 10.5" x 5.5". *Courtesy of the Donald and Marsha Levine Ceramics and Glass Collection at the Sands Point Preserve, Sands Point, N.Y.* $700-800.

Vase (1202), yellow green (dip, with engine turning), *"Dancing Hours,"* mark: WEDGWOOD, ca. 1870, 10. 5" x 5". *Courtesy of the Kerner Collection.* $800-1000.

Vase (1202), black (dip, with engine turning), *"Dancing Hours,"* mark: WEDGWOOD, ENGLAND, ca. 1900, 10.25" x 5". *Courtesy of the Kerner Collection.* $800-1000.

Vase (1202), sage green (dip, with engine turning), *"Dancing Hours,"* mark: WEDGWOOD, ENGLAND, ca. 1900, 10.25" x 4.75". *Courtesy of the Kerner Collection.* $700-900.

Vase (1202), sage green (dip), *"Dancing Hours,"* mark: WEDGWOOD, ca. 1880, 11" x 5.5". *Courtesy of the Kerner Collection.* $800-1000.

Vase (1202), tricolor (dip, sage green and pale blue), *"Dancing Hours,"* mark: WEDGWOOD, ENGLAND, ca. 1900, 11" x 5.5". *Courtesy of the Kerner Collection.* $1200-1500.

Leda and the Swan Vases

First made in the 1780s, this is an exquisite vase with swan handles and a stunning finial that depicts the coupling of Leda and Jupiter in the guise of a swan. The progeny of this union was Helen of Troy and the heavenly twins, Castor and Pollux. The examples shown here were all made from the eighteenth to the early nineteenth centuries. This particular vase shape is extremely rare and is highly sought after by collectors of first period Wedgwood Jasper. A reproduction was issued in a limited edition of 100 in the year 2000 as part of the Wedgwood Masterpiece collection

Vase (274 – Leda and the Swan)), dark blue (dip), mark: WEDGWOOD, ca.1810, 11.5" x 6.5". *Courtesy of the Buten Collection of Wedgwood at the Sands Point Preserve, Sands Point, N.Y.* \$4000-5000.

Vase (274 – Leda and the Swan), pale blue (dip, on non-original white base), mark: WEDGWOOD, 18th century, 10.25" h. *Courtesy of Skinner, Inc., Boston and Bolton, Ma.* \$3000-4000.

Lid and finial of previous item.

Vase (274 – Leda and the Swan), lilac (dip), mar: WEDGWOOD, ca. 1820, 11.5" x 6.5". *Anonymous Private Collection.* $7500-9500.

Monopodia Vases

This type of Jasper vase derives its name from the one foot (monopodia) that supports the columns with the lion headed tops. It is a superb design with floral festoons, cameos, and other ornamentation. They have been produced in many colors as well as tricolor combinations mostly in the late nineteenth century. This is another example of a very special shape that most collectors would love to have in their collections.

Vase (Monopodia – 1184), tricolor (solid, white with dark blue and yellow relief), mark: WEDGWOOD, ca. 1870, 7.25" x 4.5". *Courtesy of Jeffrey S. Milkins.* $3000-4000.

Vase (Monopodia - 1184), tricolor (dip, lilac and sage green), *"Cupids and Goat,"* mark: WEDGWOOD, ca. 1880, 5.25" x 3.75". *Courtesy of Edward L. Knowles.* $1200-1500.

Vase (Monopodia – 1184), tricolor, (solid, white with lilac and sage green relief), mark: WEDGWOOD, ca. 1875, 7" x 5.5". *Anonymous Private Collection.* $2500-3500.

Vase (Monopodia – 1184), pale blue (solid), mark: WEDGWOOD, ENGLAND, ca. 1895, 6.75" x 4.25". *Courtesy of the Kerner Collection.* $800-1000.

Vase (Monopodia - 1184), tricolor (dip, sage green and lilac), *"Cupids at Play,"* mark: WEDGWOOD, ca. 1880, 6.75" x 5". *Courtesy of Edward L. Knowles.* $1200-1500.

Moon Flasks

This is by far the most uncharacteristic Wedgwood Jasper vase. It was introduced in the 1870s and reflects the then strong influence that Japanese art was having in the Western World. Its disparate design elements, which include classical cameos as well as prunus plants, do not add up to a pleasing whole, but this does not keep it from commanding a high price whenever it is offered for sale. The name "Moon Flask" derives from its almost circular shape.

Vase (Moon Flask), chocolate brown (dip), mark: WEDGWOOD, early 20th century, 5.5" h. *Courtesy of Skinner, Inc., Boston and Bolton, Ma.* $2500-3500.

Vase (Moon Flask), tricolor (dip, sage green and lilac), mark: WEDGWOOD, ca. 1875, 6" x 5.5". *Courtesy of Elizabeth and Paul Lauer.* $1500-1800.

Pair of Vases (Moon Flasks), tricolor (dip, pale blue and lilac), mark: WEDGWOOD, ca. 1875, 5.25" x 5.25". *Anonymous Private Collection.* $3000-4000.

Pegasus Vases

These classic vases are surely among the finest ever made by Wedgwood in Jasper. Named for its Pegasus finial, many impressive elements (including Medusa masks) characterize this very special vase shape that was modeled by John Flaxman Jr. and produced by Wedgwood in 1786. Its bas-relief image is entitled "Apotheosis of Homer." In the following year a subsequent version was made showing the very complementary "Apotheosis of Virgil." The Pegasus Vase has been reissued over the centuries and is often seen on quite elaborate plinths or drum bases. Also included here is another shape vase that also has the Pegasus finial. The original version and its reproductions are also known as the Homer Vase.

Vase (Pegasus), black (dip), *"Apotheosis of Virgil,"* mark: WEDGWOOD, early 19th century, 18.25" h. *Courtesy of Skinner, Inc., Boston and Bolton, Ma.* $8000-10,000.

Vase (Pegasus) on drum base, black (dip), *"Apotheosis of Virgil,"* mark: WEDGWOOD, ca. 1800, 28.5" x 10". *Courtesy of Elizabeth and Paul Lauer.* $20,000-25,000.

Vase (Pegasus) on plinth, black (dip), *"Apotheosis of Homer,"* mark: WEDGWOOD, ca. 1880, 24.5" x 10". *Courtesy of Elizabeth and Paul Lauer.* $15,000-20,000.

Vase (Pegasus), pale blue (dip), "Apotheosis of Virgil," mark: WEDGWOOD, 1910 (stamped "Made for Mr. Charles Bellows"), 19" x 10". *Courtesy of Edward L. Knowles.* $8000-10,000.

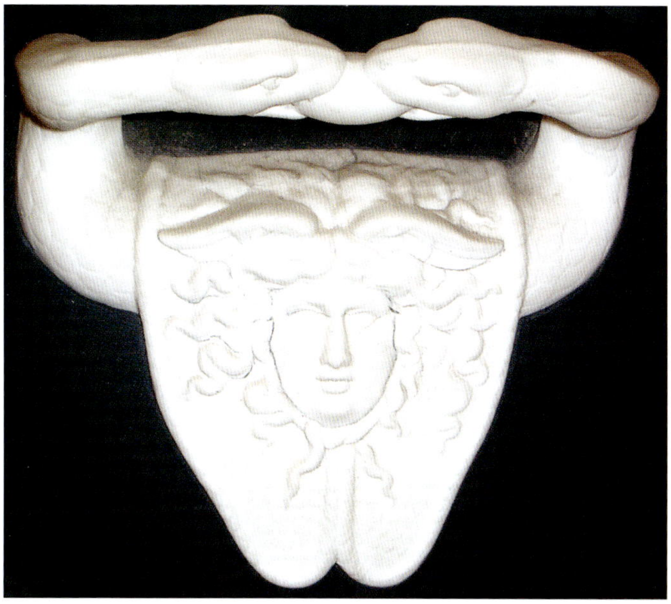

Detail of Pegasus Vases, *"Medusa Mask"*.

Detail of Pegasus Vases, *"Pegasus Finial"*.

Vase, pale blue (solid, with Pegasus finial), *"Apollo and the Muses,"* mark: WEDGWOOD, ca. 1785, 15.75" h. *Courtesy of Skinner, Inc., Boston and Bolton, Ma.* $5500-7500.

Portland Vases

If there is any one object that is synonymous with Wedgwood it must certainly be the Portland Vase. Its history has been very extensively documented so it will only be briefly summarized here. Based on a glass original from the reign of the Roman Emperor Augustus (27BC-14AD) and known as the Barberini vase, Wedgwood and several of his modelers, including William Hackwood, worked for four years to produce a Jasper copy of this ancient masterpiece. The first successful copy was presented in 1789 and at least 25 of the so-called "first edition" or "original" copies are known to exist. Many subsequent editions of varying colors and sizes have been made up to contemporary times. Shown here are examples of Portland Vases from several centuries, including one of Josiah Wedgwood's original copies as well as some very recent versions. There has always been considerable controversy about the subjects depicted on the Portland vase and a definitive answer has never been agreed upon, although one popular theory relates the frieze to the story of Peleus and Thetis, the parents of Achilles, who may also be depicted with Helen of Troy on the opposite side. The base image is thought to be the head of Paris and is usually found on full size copies only.

Portland Vase, black (solid), mark: WEDGWOOD, ca. 1790 (First Edition, #22), 10.25" x 6.5. *Courtesy of Elizabeth and Paul Lauer.* Very rare.

Portland Vase, black (solid), mark: WEDGWOOD, ca. 1875-80 ("Northwood" Edition modeled by Thomas Lovett), 10.25" x 6.5". *Courtesy of Elizabeth and Paul Lauer.* $25,000-30,000.

Portland Vase, dark blue (dip), mark: WEDGWOOD, ca. 1880, 10.5" x 8". *Anonymous Private Collection.* $1500-2000.

Portland Vase, lilac (dip), mark: WEDGWOOD, ca. 1880, 6" x 4". *Courtesy of Ellen Rubell.* $1800-2000.

Portland Vase, yellow (dip), mark: WEDGWOOD, ca. 1900, 7" h. *Courtesy of Skinner, Inc., Boston and Bolton, Ma.* $1200-1500.

Portland Vase, pale blue (dip), mark: WEDG-WOOD, ENGLAND, ca. 1900, 8" x 4.75". *Courtesy of the Kerner Collection.* $800-1000.

Portland Vase, crimson (dip), mark: WEDGWOOD, ENGLAND, ca. 1925, 4" x 3.25". *Courtesy of David Kroun.* $1500-2000.

Portland Vase, sage green (dip), mark: WEDGWOOD, ENGLAND, ca. 1905, 10.25" x 5.5". *Courtesy of the Buten Collection of Wedgwood at the Sands Point Preserve, Sands Point, N.Y.* $1500-1800.

Portland Vase, olive green (dip), mark: WEDGWOOD, ENGLAND, ca. 1930, 5" x 3". *Courtesy of the Kerner Collection.* $600-800.

Portland Vase, white (solid, with pale blue relief), mark: WEDGWOOD, MADE IN ENGLAND, 1981 (limited edition of 50), 10.25" x 8". *Courtesy of Jeffrey S. Milkins.* $2700-3000.

Portland Vase, cane yellow (solid, with black relief), mark: WEDGWOOD, MADE IN ENGLAND, 1999 (limited edition of 50), 6" x 4". *Courtesy of Elizabeth and Paul Lauer.* $800-1000.

Torch Vases

Named by collectors for its immediately recognizable design that somewhat resembles strapware, this striking vase was produced in several colors as well as tricolor versions and is often capped by a very elegant and delicate lovebirds finial sitting on a pierced lid. This delicacy probably explains why so many surviving copies of this vase are offered without their lids. The examples shown here all date from the nineteenth century.

Vase (Torch – 393, missing lid), tricolor (solid, white with pale blue and sage green relief), mark: WEDGWOOD, early 19th century, 6.75" h. . *Courtesy of Skinner, Inc., Boston and Bolton, Ma.* $1200-1500.

Vase (Torch – 393) with pierced lid and lovebird finial), pale blue (dip), mark: WEDGWOOD, 1860, 7" x 4.5". *Anonymous Private Collection.* $1200-1500.

Vase (Torch – 393) with pierced lid and lovebird finial), pale blue (dip), mark: WEDGWOOD, ca. 1880, 7.25" x 4". *Courtesy of the Kerner Collection.* $800-1000.

Tripod Vases

The Tripod vase shape gets its name for obvious reasons and is another classic type that was first produced in Jasper during the closing decades of the eighteenth century. When fitted with a special cover that can be inverted some versions can also serve as candleholders and are known as cassolettes. On display here are several very distinct types, including one very early version with diceware ornamentation and a late nineteenth century tricolor example.

Pair of Cassolettes (Tripod Vases with Candleholders), pale blue (solid), mark: WEDGWOOD, ca. 1790, 11" x 5.75". *Courtesy of Edward L. Knowles.* $5000-7000.

Vase (Tripod with Candleholder), diceware (dip, bright blue with yellow quatrefoils), mark: WEDGWOOD, ca. 1790, 9.75" x 4". *Anonymous Private Collection.* $8000-10,000.

Vase (Tripod), pale lilac (dip), mark: WEDGWOOD, ca. 1800, 8.5" x 4.5". *Courtesy of Ellen Rubell.* $1800-2000.

Vase (Tripod), tricolor (solid, white with lilac and sage green relief), mark: WEDG-WOOD, ca. 1880, 8" x 5.5". *Courtesy of Elizabeth and Paul Lauer.* $3000-4000.

Trophy Vases

The Trophy Vase derives its name from the trophies that form part of its relief work. This is one of the most frequently seen types of Jasper vase and it has been available in many colors and tricolor combinations. It has also been offered in a vast range of sizes from a few inches to well over a foot and a half tall. Shown here are a couple of freestanding pairs, but they are just as often offered standing on plinths. They have been made in Jasper probably since the early nineteenth century and they were still being produced in the late twentieth.

Pair of Vases (Trophy – 350), tricolor (dip, dark blue and sage green), *"Muses,"* mark: WEDGWOOD, mid-19th century, 11" h. *Courtesy of Skinner, Inc., Boston and Bolton, Ma.* $3000-5000.

Pair of Vases (Trophy – 350 – Miniature), sage green (dip), *"The Procession," and "Domestic Employment,"* mark: WEDGWOOD, ca. 1880, 3" x 1. 5". *Courtesy of Dr. and Mrs. Victor Polikoff.* $1200-1500.

Zodiac Vases

This group of vases that bear the Wedgwood factory shape number of 372 or 505 are notable for having the twelve signs of the zodiac as part of their relief ornamentation. These particular representations of the zodiac were first made for Wedgwood in 1776 by Mary Landré and later remodeled by Hackwood. These are very striking examples of late nineteenth century vases and the zodiac motifs are perfectly compatible with the other design elements.

Vase (Zodiac – 372), black (solid), *"Terpsichore,"* mark: WEDGWOOD, ca. 1870, 9.5" x 5". *Courtesy of the Kerner Collection.* $1200-1500.

Vase (Zodiac - 372). tricolor (solid, white with white, sage green and lilac relief), *"Polymnia,"* mark: WEDGWOOD, ca. 1870), 9" x 6". *Courtesy of Jeffrey S. Milkins.* $2500-3500.

Vase (Zodiac - 372), sage green (dip), *"Euterpe,"* mark: WEDGWOOD, ENGLAND, ca. 1900, 12" x 7". *Courtesy of the Buten Collection of Wedgwood at the Sands Point Preserve, Sands Point, N.Y.* $2000-3000.

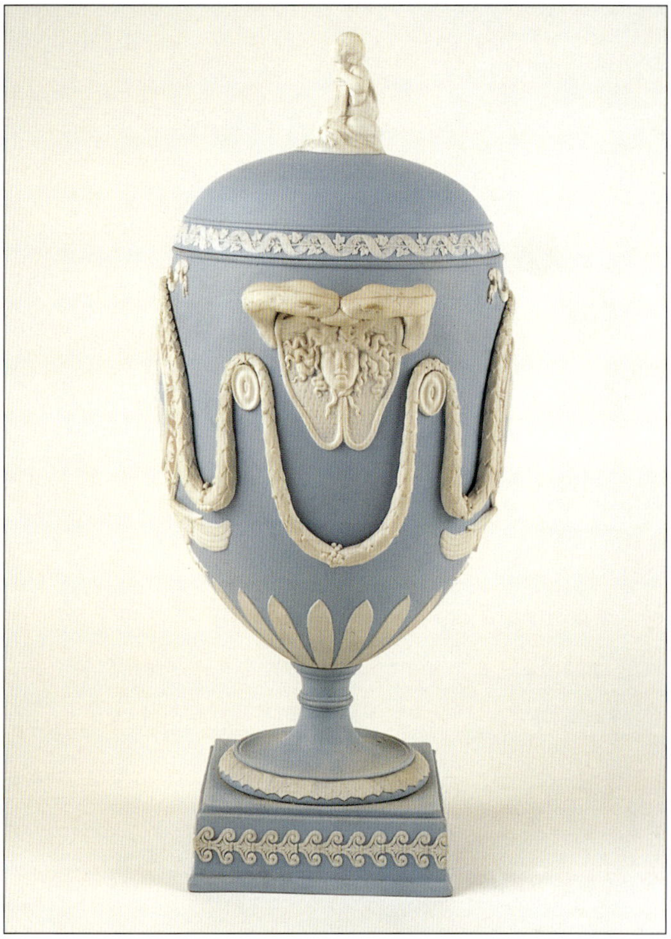

Vase (Zodiac – 505), tricolor (dip, pale blue and lilac), *"Zephyrs,"* mark: WEDGWOOD, ca. 1865, 12.75" x 5.5". *Anonymous Private Collection.* $4000-6000.

Miscellaneous Vases: Part I (with names or numbers)

Shown in this group of photos is a large array of vases all of which are known by a name or a Wedgwood factory shape number that has been found by the author. Most of the shape numbers were found in one of several Wedgwood shape books located in the Buten Library. These books contain hand drawn illustrations in numerical order of Wedgwood products of all types. Unfortunately there were a number of large gaps in these books, so the shape numbers of many vases could not be ascertained. However, a few additional numbers were found as they were incised by hand on the undersides of particular vases. The vases with names are listed first in alphabetical order followed by those with numbers in numerical order.

Vase (Apollo), pale blue (dip, with Apollo finial), mark: WEDGWOOD, MADE IN ENGLAND, 1930 (designed by John Goodwin to commemorate the 200th anniversary of the birth of Josiah Wedgwood), 8.75" h. ". *Courtesy of Skinner, Inc., Boston and Bolton, Ma.* $1000-1200.

Vase (Cameo), tricolor (solid, pale blue and lilac), mark: WEDGWOOD, ca. 1860, 6" x 2.5", *Anonymous Private Collection*. $800-1000.

Vase (Blind Man's Buff), sage green (solid, with Cupid finial), mark: WEDGWOOD, MADE IN ENGLAND, 1998 (limited edition stamped "Blind Man's Buff Vase,"), 12" x 4". *Courtesy of David Kroun*. $700-800.

Vase (Leopard Tripod – 1574), pale blue (solid, with engine turning), mark: WEDG-WOOD, early 19th century, 11.5" h. *Courtesy of Skinner, Inc., Boston and Bolton, Ma.* $10,000-15,000.

Vase (Parnassus - 3065), pale blue (solid), *"Terpsichore,"* mark: WEDGWOOD, MADE IN ENGLAND, 1972, 7.75" x 4.5". *Courtesy of the Kerner Collection.* $200-300.

Vase (Michelangelo - 180), pale blue (dip, with three white caryatid supporters), mark: WEDGWOOD, ca. 1800, 13.25" h. *Courtesy of Skinner, Inc., Boston and Bolton, Ma.* $10,000-15,000.

Vase (Parnassus - 3065) white (solid, with sage green relief), mark: WEDGWOOD, MADE IN ENGLAND, 1976, 8" x 4.5", *Courtesy of Mary and Peter Rockefeller.* $300-400.

Vase (Tricorner), sage green (dip), *"Herculaneum Figure,"* mark: WEDGWOOD, mid-19th century, 8.325" h. *Courtesy of Skinner, Inc., Boston and Bolton, Ma.* $600-800.

Vase (11), tricolor (dip), black and yellow-buff with engine turning, mark: WEDGWOOD, ENGLAND, ca. 1930, 13" x 6.5". *Courtesy of Edward L. Knowles.* $7000-9000.

Tripod Goat Vase (281), pale blue (solid), 8.5" x 6". *Anonymous Private Collection.* $7500-9500.

Pair of Vases (30), tricolor (solid, white with sage green and lilac relief), mark: WEDGWOOD, mid-19th century, 14" h. *Courtesy of Skinner, Inc., Boston and Bolton, Ma.* $1800-2000.

Vase (26), black (dip, with engine turning), mark: WEDGWOOD, MADE IN ENGLAND, 1963, 8.5" x 4.25". *Courtesy of the Kerner Collection.* $600-800.

Vase (26), lilac (dip, with engine turning), mark: WEDGWOOD, MADE IN ENGLAND, 1961, 8.5" x 5.5". *Anonymous Private Collection.* $800-900.

Vase (40), tricolor (solid, white with lilac and sage green relief), *"Melpomene,"* mark: WEDGWOOD, MADE IN ENGLAND, c.1985, 12" x 6". *Anonymous Private Collection.* $900-1000.

Two Vases (117), dark blue (dip), marks: WEDGWOOD, WVO =1860 or 1886, WEDGWOOD, WUQ = 1862 or 1888, 5.75" x 3.5" and 6.5" x 4.25". *Courtesy of the Buten Collection of Wedgwood at the Sands Point Preserve, Sands Point, N.Y.* $1000-1200.

Vase on Plinth, sage green (dip), *"Cupids" and "Zephyr,"* mark: WEDGWOOD, late 19th century, 13.125". *Courtesy of Skinner, Inc., Boston and Bolton, Ma.* $2000-3000.

Vase (Hanging – 137), dark blue (dip), *"Polymnia" and "Apollo,"* mark: WEDGWOOD, ca. 1840, 9.5" X 5.75". *Anonymous Private Collection.* $1000-1200.

Vase (171), pale blue (solid), mark: WEDGWOOD, ca. 1886, 9.375" x 5". *Courtesy of the Buten Collection of Wedgwood at the Sands Point Preserve, Sands Point, N.Y.* $1000-1200.

Vase (174), tricolor (dip, lilac and pale blue), *"Sacrifice Figures,"* mark: WEDGWOOD, ca. 1880, 8.75" h. *Courtesy of Skinner, Inc., Boston and Bolton, Ma.* $1000-1200.

Vase (174), dark blue (dip), mark: WEDGWOOD + "mustache marks," c.1820, 9.5" x 4.25". *Courtesy of Adele Ierubino Barnett.* $700-800.

Vase (174), tricolor (solid, light blue and lilac), *"Hercules Strangling the Nemean Lion,"* mark: WEDGWOOD, late 19th century, 9.5" h. *Courtesy of Skinner, Inc., Boston and Bolton, Ma.* $1600-1800.

Vase (264), black (dip), *"Bacchanalian Boys at Play,"* mark: WEDGWOOD, mid-19th century, 7.625" h. *Courtesy of Skinner, Inc., Boston and Bolton, Ma.* $1000-1200.

Vase (174), four color (dip, black, yellow and dark blue), *"Classical Figures,"* mark: WEDGWOOD, ENGLAND, ca. 1900, 8.25" h. *Courtesy of Skinner, Inc., Boston and Bolton, Ma.* $3000-4000.

Vase (264), lilac (dip), *"Boys at Play,"* mark: WEDGWOOD, ca. 1880, 7.5" x 4.25". *Courtesy of Ellen Rubell.* $1800-2000.

Vase (Orange Peel – 264), pale sage green, *"Procession of Cupids,"* mark: WEDGWOOD, ca. 1790, 9" x 4". *Anonymous Private Collection.* $2500-3000.

Vase (264), tricolor (solid, white with sage green and lilac relief), mark: WEDGWOOD, ca. 1885, 7" h. *Courtesy of Skinner, Inc., Boston and Bolton, Ma.* $1200-1500.

Vase (264), pale blue (solid), *"Muses,"* mark: WEDGWOOD, MADE IN ENGLAND, 1960, 10.5" x 5". *Courtesy of the Kerner Collection.* $500-600.

Vase (266) with Snake Handles), diceware (dip, sage green with yellow quatrefoils), *"Marriage of Cupid and Psyche,"* mark: WEDGWOOD, ca. 1790, 14.75" x 6.5". *Courtesy of Jeffrey S. Milkins.* $5000-7000.

Vase (266) with Snake Handles on Pedestal, pale blue (solid), *"Domestic Employment" and "Sacrifice Figure,"* mark: WEDGWOOD, ca. 1790, 22.75" x. 5.25". *Courtesy of Edward L. Knowles.* $5000-7000.

Vase (266) on Pedestal, pale blue (solid), *"Domestic Employment" and "Sacrifice Figure,"* mark: WEDGWOOD, ca. 1790, 21.5" x. 5.25". *Courtesy of Edward L. Knowles.* $3000-4000.

Vase (266 - missing lid) with lion mask handles, sage green (dip), *"Sacrifice Figures,"* mark: WEDGWOOD, early 19th century, 10.5" h. *Courtesy of Stamford Auction, Stamford, Ct.* $800-1000.

Vase (268), pale blue (solid), mark: WEDGWOOD, 18th century, 6.5" h. *Courtesy of Skinner, Inc., Boston and Bolton, Ma.* $1000-1200.

Vase (271), sage green (dip), *"Bellerophon Watering Pegasus,"* mark: WEDGWOOD, ca. 1880, *Courtesy of Elizabeth and Paul Lauer.* 8" x 5.25". $800-1000.

Vase (275), tricolor (dip, sage green and pale blue), *"Muses,"* mark: WEDGWOOD, late 19th century, 9.5" h. *Courtesy of Skinner, Inc., Boston and Bolton, Ma.* $1800-2000.

Vase (271), black (dip), *"Bellerophon Watering Pegasus,"* mark: WEDGWOOD, ca. 1880, *Courtesy of the Kerner Collection.* 8" x 5.25". $800-1000.

Pair of Vases (289), pale blue (solid), *"Apollo," etc.*, mark: WEDGWOOD, ca. 1860, 7.5" x 4.75". *Courtesy of Elizabeth and Paul Lauer.* $1500-1800 (pair).

Vase (289), black (dip), *"Hope and the Anchor,"* mark: WEDGWOOD, early 19th century, 6" h. *Courtesy of Skinner, Inc., Boston and Bolton, Ma.* $700-900.

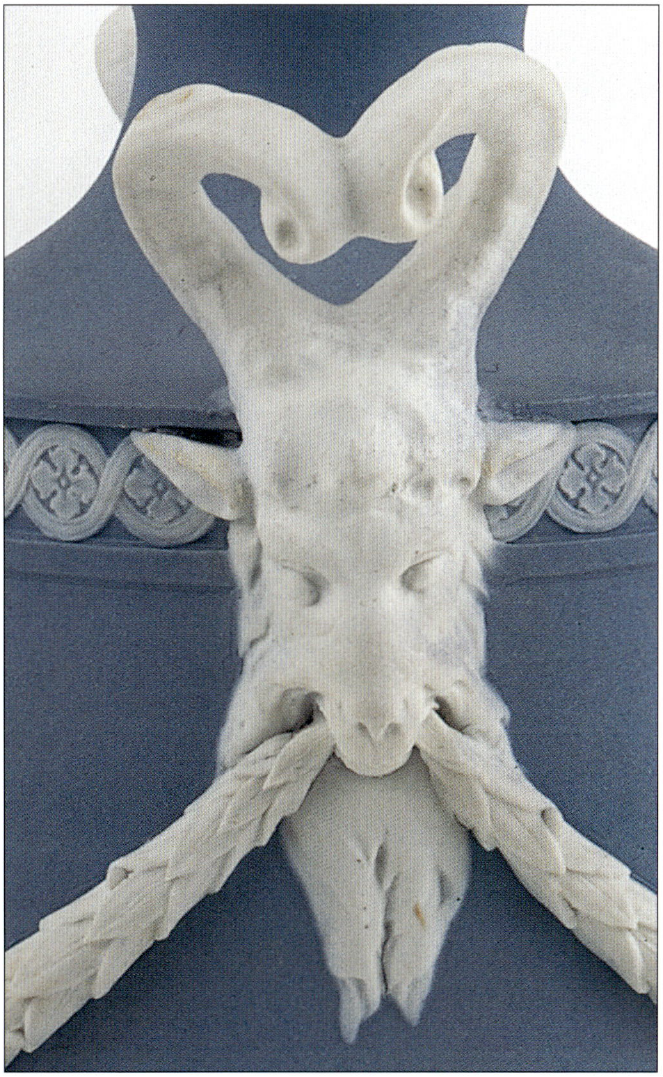

Detail of above item: *"Goat Mask"*.

Vase (289), tricolor (solid, white with sage green and lilac relief), *"War and Peace,"* mark: WEDGWOOD, ENGLAND, ca. 1900, 7.625" h. *Courtesy of Skinner, Inc., Boston and Bolton, Ma.* $1200-1500.

Vase (289), four color (dip, yellow, black, dark blue), *"Andromache,"* mark: WEDGWOOD, ca. 1880, 6" x 4". *Courtesy of Dr. and Mrs. Victor Polikoff.* $3000-4000.

Vase (294), lilac (dip), *"Nike and the Warrior,"* mark: WEDGWOOD, ca. 1880, 8" x 4.5". *Courtesy of Ellen Rubell.* $1200-1500.

Pair of Potpourri Vases (369), pale blue (solid), *"Muses,"* mark: WEDGWOOD, ca. 1862, 10.75" h. *Courtesy of Skinner, Inc., Boston and Bolton, Ma.* $3500-4500.

Vase (298), pale lilac (dip, with cupid finial), *"Hercules in the Garden of the Hersperides,"* mark: WEDGWOOD, ca. 1800, 11.375" h. *Courtesy of Skinner, Inc., Boston and Bolton, Ma.* $1200-1500.

Vase (372), diceware (dip, sage green with lilac quatrefoils), *"Sacrifice Figures,"* mark: WEDGWOOD, mid 19th century, 9.5" h. *Courtesy of Skinner, Inc., Boston and Bolton, Ma.* $2500-3500.

Pair of Vases (352), dark blue (dip), *"Sportive Love" and "Aesculapius,"* mark: WEDGWOOD, late 19th century, 6" h. *Courtesy of Skinner, Inc., Boston and Bolton, Ma.* $800-1000.

Vase (372), diceware (dip, black with yellow quatrefoils), *"Boys at Play,"* mark: WEDGWOOD, mid-19th century, 12.675" h. *Courtesy of Skinner, Inc., Boston and Bolton, Ma.* $2500-3500.

Vase (382) with Frog, black (dip), mark: WEDGWOOD, ca. 1860, 8" x 4.5". *Courtesy of the Buten Collection of Wedgwood at the Sands Point Preserve, Sands Point, N.Y.* $800-1000.

Vase (372), diceware (dip, sage green with yellow quatrefoils), *"Boys at Play,"* mark: WEDGWOOD, ca. 1880, 13" x 6". *Courtesy of Jeffrey S. Milkins.* $2500-3500.

Vase (384) with Frog, tricolor (dip, yellow with pale blue relief), *"Cupid as Spring,"* mark: WEDGWOOD, mid-19th century, 5" h. *Courtesy of Skinner, Inc., Boston and Bolton, Ma.* $1500-1800.

Vase (384), sage green (dip, with white trellis ornamentation), mark: WEDGWOOD, mid-19th century, 6.25" h. *Courtesy of Skinner, Inc., Boston and Bolton, Ma.* $900-1100.

Vase (384) with Frog, yellow buff (dip, with black relief), *"Sacrifice Figures,"* mark: WEDGWOOD, ENGLAND, ca. 1930, 8" x 7". *Courtesy of the Kerner Collection.* $800-1000.

Vase (388), diceware (dip, light blue with green quatrefoils and brass mountings), *"Sacrifice Figures,"* mark: WEDGWOOD, ca. 1870, 12" x 5.5". *Anonymous Private Collection.* $10,000-12,000.

Vase (384), dark blue (dip, with star and fern pattern), mark: WEDGWOOD, ca. 1890, 8" x 7". *Anonymous Private Collection.* $800-1000.

Vase (388), diceware (dip, sage green with dark blue quatrefoils), mark: WEDGWOOD, ca. 1880, 8" x 4.25". *Anonymous Private Collection.* $2000-3000.

Vase (388), diceware (dip, black with yellow quatrefoils), "*Sacrifice Figures,*" mark: WEDGWOOD, ca. 1860, 11.5" x 5.75". *Courtesy of Dr. and Mrs. Victor Polikoff.* $5000-7000.

Vase (394), yellow buff (dip, with black relief), mark: WEDGWOOD, ENGLAND, ca. 1930, 8" h. *Courtesy of Skinner, Inc., Boston and Bolton, Ma.* $600-800.

Pair of Vases (395), yellow buff (dip, with black relief), mark: WEDG-WOOD, ENGLAND, ca. 1930, 5" h. *Courtesy of Skinner, Inc., Boston and Bolton, Ma.* $800-1000.

Vase (443), pale blue (solid) with Cupid finial, mark: WEDGWOOD, ca. 1880, 9" x 5". *Courtesy of Edward L. Knowles.* $1500-1800.

Vase (439) on Drum Base, dark blue (dip), *"Classical Figures,"* mark: WEDGWOOD, early 19th century, 18.625" h. *Courtesy of Skinner, Inc., Boston and Bolton, Ma.* $2500-3500.

Vase (443), black (dip), mark: WEDGWOOD BB, ca. 1900 (modeled by Bert Bentley), 8.5" x 5". *Courtesy of Dr. and Mrs. Victor Polikoff* $1500-2500.

Vase (819), tricolor (solid, white with lilac and sage relief), *"Antonia,"* mark: WEDGWOOD, ca. 1880, 5.875" x 4". *Courtesy of Elizabeth and Paul Lauer.* $2000-3000.

Vase (443), tricolor (solid, lilac with sage green and white relief), mark: WEDGWOOD, MADE IN ENGLAND, 1989, (limited edition of 100 from St. James Collection), 8.5" x 4.25". *Anonymous Private Collection.* $900-1000.

Vase (905), dark blue (dip), *"Personification of the River Thames,"* mark: WEDGWOOD, ca. 1890, 6.5" x 4.75". *Anonymous Private Collection.* $700-900.

Pair of Vases (932), dark blue (dip), *"Apollo" and "Sacrifice Figure,"* mark: WEDGWOOD, ca. 1890, 4" x 3.25". *Author's Collection.* $350-450 (each).

Vase (943), pale blue (dip), *"Blind Man's Buff,"* mark: WEDGWOOD, mid-19th century, 6.5" h. ". *Courtesy of Skinner, Inc., Boston and Bolton, Ma.* $500-700.

Vase (953) with white scroll handles, dark blue (dip), *"Muses,"* mark: WEDGWOOD, late 19th century, 7" h. *Courtesy of Skinner, Inc., Boston and Bolton, Ma.* $700-900.

Vase (953 – miniature), dark blue (dip), *"Priam Begging the Body of Hector from Achilles,"* mark: WEDGWOOD, ca. 1880, 1.5" x 1.25. *Author's Collection.* $500-600.

Three Vases (953, plain handles, no handles, lion (?) mask handles), dark blue (dip), *"The Archers," " Cupid Disarmed," " Apollo Musagetes,"* marks: WEDGWOOD, ca. 1880-1890, 3" x 2.5", 3.5" x 2.5", 3.5" x 3.25". *Author's Collection.* $300-400, $250-350, $400-500.

Vase (953 with white lion head handles), dark blue (dip), mark: WEDGWOOD, ca. 1880, 4" x 4". *Courtesy of David Kroun.* $500-600.

Vase (953) with "Bat" Handles, sage green (dip), mark: WEDGWOOD, ca. 1890, 5" X 5.5". *Courtesy of the Buten Collection of Wedgwood at the Sands Point Preserve, Sands Point, N.Y.* $700-800.

Vase (1002), dark blue (dip), *"Psyche Bound to a Tree by Cupids,"* mark: WEDGWOOD, ca.1890, 3.25" x 4". *Anonymous Private Collection.* $400-500.

Vase (1011), dark blue (dip), "Coriolanus," mark: WEDGWOOD, ca. 1880, 5.5 x 4.25". *Courtesy of David Kroun.* $800-900.

Pair of Vases (1009) on Drum Bases, dark blue (dip), *"Fame"* and *"Aesculapius,"*
mark: WEDGWOOD, mid-19th century, 14.25" h. *Courtesy of Skinner, Inc., Boston and Bolton, Ma.* $1000-1200.

Vase (1015), sage green (dip), *"Muses Watering Pegasus,"* mark: WEDGWOOD, ca. 1890, 7" X 4.5". *Anonymous Private Collection.* $800-1000.

Vase (1023), black (dip, with engine turning), *"Sportive Love,"* mark: Wedgwood, early 19th century, 9.25" h. *Courtesy of Skinner, Inc., Boston and Bolton, Ma.* $900-1100.

Vase (1025), black (dip), *"Domestic Employment,"* mark: WEDGWOOD, ca. 1800, 9" x 4. 5". *Courtesy of Dr. and Mrs. Victor Polikoff.* $2000-3000.

Vase (1025), white (solid,with sage green and lilac relief), *"A Sacrifice,"* mark: WEDGWOOD, ca. 1870, 6.25" x 4.5". *Courtesy of Dr. and Mrs. Victor Polikoff.* $1800-2000.

Vase (1025), white (solid, with pale blue relief), mark: WEDGWOOD, ca. 1880, 6.5" x 2.5", *Courtesy of Adele Ierubino Barnett.* $1000-1200.

Vase (1033), sage green (dip), *"Cupid Stringing His Bow,"* mark: WEDGWOOD, early 19th century, 17" h. *Courtesy of Skinner, Inc., Boston and Bolton, Ma.* $1200-1500.

Vase (1108), black (dip), mark: WEDGWOOD, ENGLAND, ca. 1895, 7" x 4". *Anonymous Private Collection.* $800-1000.

Pair of Vases (1035), pale blue (solid), "Muses," mark: WEDGWOOD, AAQ = 1862 or 1888, 6.5" x 4.5". *Courtesy of the Donald and Marsha Levine Ceramics and Glass Collection at the Sands Point Preserve, Sands Point, N.Y.* $3000-5000.

Pair of Vases (1055), tricolor (solid, white with sage green and lilac relief), mark: WEDG-WOOD, mid-19th century, 11.625" h. *Courtesy of Skinner, Inc., Boston and Bolton, Ma.* $1800-2000.

Vase (1200) with Pierced Lid, tricolor (dip, dark blue and lilac), *"Cupid with Club of Hercules,"* mark: WEDGWOOD, ca. 1875, 12" x 7". *Courtesy of Edward L. Knowles.* $3000-4000.

Pair of Vases (1195) on bases, tricolor (solid, pale blue with lilac medallions), *"Apollo and Bacchus," etc.*, mark: WEDGWOOD, ca. 1800, 16" x 6.25". *Courtesy of Edward L. Knowles.* $4000-6000.

Pair of Vases (1200) with Pierced Lids, tricolor (dip, pale blue and lilac), *"Cupids,"* mark: WEDGWOOD, mid-19th century, 12" h. *Courtesy of Skinner, Inc., Boston and Bolton, Ma.* $5000-7000.

Vase (1195), tricolor (dip, sage green and lilac), *"Henrietta Finch,"* mark: WEDGWOOD, ca. 1880, 10.5" x 6". *Courtesy of the Kerner Collection.* $1200-1500.

Vase (1200) with Pierced Lid, tricolor (solid, white with sage green and lilac relief), *"Dipping of Achilles,"* mark: WEDGWOOD, late 19th century, 13.25" h. *Courtesy of Skinner, Inc., Boston and Bolton, Ma.* $2500-3500.

Vase (1200), tricolor (dip, lilac and pale blue), *"Sacrifice Figure,"* mark: WEDGWOOD, ENGLAND, ca. 1900, 8.375" h. *Courtesy of Skinner, Inc., Boston and Bolton, Ma.* $1800-2000.

Vase (1200) with Pierced Lid, lilac (solid), mark: WEDGWOOD, MADE IN ENGLAND, *"Melpomene,"* mark: WEDGWOOD, MADE IN ENGLAND, ca. 1980, 12" x 5.5". *Anonymous Private Collection.* $900-1000.

Vase (1271), sage green (dip, with lovebirds finial), mark: WEDGWOOD, mid-19th century, 7.25" h. *Courtesy of Skinner, Inc., Boston and Bolton, Ma.* $900-1100. $600-800.

Vase (1316), pale blue (solid), *"Blind Man's Buff,"* mark: WEDGWOOD, 18th century, 10.75" h. *Courtesy of Skinner, Inc., Boston and Bolton, Ma.* $1200-1500.

Vase (1316), pale blue (solid), *"Infant Academy,"* mark: WEDGWOOD, ca. 1790, 13.5" x 6.75". *Courtesy of the Kerner Collection.* $2500-3500.

Pair of Vases (1316) on Plinths, pale sage green, *"Muses,"* mark: WEDGWOOD, 19th century, 11.5" h. *Courtesy of Skinner, Inc., Boston and Bolton, Ma.* $2500-3500.

Vase (1316), terra cotta (solid), *"Muses,"* mark: WEDGWOOD, MADE IN ENGLAND, 1956, 11.75" x 7". *Anonymous Private Collection.* $700-800.

Vase (1316), dark blue (dip), *"Muses,"* mark: WEDGWOOD, MADE IN ENGLAND, ca. 1910, 11.75" x 6.5". *Author's Collection.* $800-1000.

Vase (1316), lilac (solid), *"Muses,"* mark: WEDGWOOD, MADE IN ENGLAND, 1961, 8.5" x 5". *Anonymous Private Collection.* $900-1000.

Vase (1399) on Pedestal, sage green (dip), *"Hercules in the Garden of the Hesperides,"* mark: WEDGWOOD, ca. 1790, 24.25" x 7.5". *Courtesy of Jeffrey S. Milkins.* $5000-7000.

Vase (1500–handles not complete), sage green (dip), *"Cupid,"* WEDGWOOD, ca. 1890, 10.25" x 4". *Anonymous Private Collection.* $1000-1200.

Vase (1626), yellow buff (dip, with black relief and engine turning), mark: WEDGWOOD, ETRURIA, ENGLAND, ca. 1895, 7" x 5.675". *Courtesy of Elizabeth and Paul Lauer.* $1200-1500.

Vase (1487), yellow (dip), *"Ulysses Staying the Chariot of Victory,"* mark: WEDGWOOD, ENGLAND, ca. 1900, 8" x 5". *Courtesy of the Kerner Collection.* $900-1000.

Vase (2068), black (solid), *"Hercules in the Garden of the Hesperides,"* mark: WEDGWOOD, ETRURIA, ENGLAND, ca. 1895, 15.5" x 8". *Courtesy of the Kerner Collection.* $1200-1500.

Vase (2068), yellow buff and black (dip), *"Hercules in the Garden of the Hesperides,"* mark: WEDGWOOD, MADE IN ENGLAND, ca. 1930, 15" x 6". ". *Courtesy of the Donald and Marsha Levine Ceramics and Glass Collection at the Sands Point Preserve, Sands Point, N.Y.* $2000-3000.

Pair of Vases (2843), yellow buff (dip, with black relief), mark: WEDGWOOD, ca. 1900, 5.75" 3.25". *Courtesy of Elizabeth and Paul Lauer.* $1000-1200 (pair).

Vase (2494), black (dip), *"Nike and the Warrior,"* mark: WEDGWOOD, early 19th century, 6.75" h. *Courtesy of Skinner, Inc., Boston and Bolton, Ma.* $1000-1200.

Miscellaneous Vases:
Part II (without names or numbers)

In this section will be found the remaining vase shapes that the author has photos of but no further names or numbers for the purpose of identification. They are shown in chronological order.

Pair of Vases, black (dip), with finials that can be turned over to become candle holders, *"Birth and Dipping of Achilles,"* mark: WEDGWOOD, ca. 1790, 10.5" x 4.5". *Anonymous Private Collection.* $10,000-12,000.

Vase, sage green (dip), *"Bacchanalian Triumph,"* mark: WEDGWOOD, ca. 1780, 17" x 8". *Courtesy of Shapiro Auctions, Australia.* $3000-4000.

Vase, pale blue (solid), *"Charlotte at the Tomb of Werther,"* mark: WEDGWOOD, ca. 1795, 10" x 4.5". ". *Courtesy of the Donald and Marsha Levine Ceramics and Glass Collection at the Sands Point Preserve, Sands Point, N.Y.* $3000-5000.

Pair of Vases, pale blue (solid), mark: WEDGWOOD, ca. 1800, 9.25" h. *Courtesy of Skinner, Inc., Boston and Bolton, Ma.* $2000-3000.

Vase, pale blue (solid, cover missing), *"Sacrifice Figures,"* mark: WEDGWOOD, 18th century, 8.25" h. *Courtesy of Skinner, Inc., Boston and Bolton, Ma.* $1000-1200.

Vase, bright blue (dip, on pale blue ground), mark: WEDGWOOD, ca. 1800, 10" x 5.5". *Courtesy of Edward L. Knowles.* $2500-3500.

Pair of Vases, pale blue (dip), *"Cupid" and "Classical Warrior,"* mark: WEDGWOOD, early 19th century, 10.5" h.. *Courtesy of Skinner, Inc., Boston and Bolton, Ma.* $2000-3000.

Vase, black (solid, missing lid), *"Cupid as Oracle, " etc.*, mark: WEDGWOOD, ca. 1800, 19" x 8". *Courtesy of the Buten Collection of Wedgwood at the Sands Point Preserve, Sands Point, N.Y.* $2500-3500.

Vase, pale blue (solid), *"Virgo,"* mark: WEDGWOOD, early19th century, 7.875" h. ". *Courtesy of Skinner, Inc., Boston and Bolton, Ma.* $500-700.

Vase, pale blue (dip, with hand sculpted floral relief), mark: WEDGWOOD, ca. 1840, 8.5" x 4.75". *Courtesy of Dr, and Mrs. Victor Polikoff.* $1200-1500.

Vase with Pierced and Insert Lids, lilac (dip), *"Boys at Play,"* mark: WEDGWOOD, mid-19th century, 8" h. *Courtesy of Skinner, Inc., Boston and Bolton, Ma.* $1200-1500.

Vase, sage green (dip), *"Domestic Employment,"* mark: WEDGWOOD, ca. 1840, 7.75" h. *Courtesy of Skinner, Inc., Boston and Bolton, Ma.* $700-900.

Vase, pale blue (dip), "Boys at Play," mark: WEDGWOOD, ca. 1860, 6.25" x 5.25, *Courtesy of Adele Ierubino Barnett.* $500-600.

Vase, pale blue (solid) with pierced cover and insert lid, *"Sacrifice Figures,"* mark: WEDGWOOD, ca. 1862, 14.25" h.. *Courtesy of Skinner, Inc., Boston and Bolton, Ma.* $1800-2000.

Vase, black (dip), mark: WEDGWOOD, ca. 1862, 6.5" h. *Courtesy of Skinner, Inc., Boston and Bolton, Ma.* $900-1100.

Pair of Vases (Goblets), dark blue (dip), "Muses," mark: WEDGWOOD, ca. 1870, 6.25" x 4". *Author's Collection.* $600-800 (each).

Vase, pale blue (solid), *"Classical Figures," etc.*, mark: WEDG-WOOD, ca. 1862, 6.625". *Courtesy of Skinner, Inc., Boston and Bolton, Ma.* $700-900.

Pair of Vases, tricolor (dip, pale blue and lilac), *"Sacrifice Figures"* and *"Sacrifice to Ceres,"* mark: WEDGWOOD, ca. 1870, 7.75" x 5". *Courtesy of Edward L. Knowles.* $2500-3500.

Pair of Vases, tricolor (dip, sage green and lilac with ormolu mounts), *"Perseus and Andromeda" and "Hercules Strangling the Nemean Lion,"* mark: WEDGWOOD ANZ = 1871, 11.35" h. *Courtesy of Skinner, Inc., Boston and Bolton, Ma.* $2000-3000.

Vase (Goblet), mark: WEDGWOOD, ca. 1880, 6" x 3.25". *Anonymous Private Collection.* $600-800.

Vase, dark blue (dip), *"Muses,"* mark: WEDGWOOD, ca. 1890, 5.25" x 3.75". *Author's Collection.* $300-400.

Vase, sage green (dip, with engine turning), *"Zephyr,"* mark: WEDGWOOD, ca. 1890, 6" x 4". *Courtesy of the Kerner Collection.* $700-900.

Vase (missing cover), dark blue (dip), *"Nike and the Warrior,"* mark: WEDGWOOD, ca. 1890, 6" x 2.75". *Courtesy of Adele Ierubino Barnett.* $300-400.

Vase, dark blue (dip), *"Dipping of Achilles,"* mark: WEDGWOOD, ENGLAND, ca. 1900, 8.5" x 4.5" *Author's Collection.* $500-600.

Vase, tricolor (dip, lilac and pale blue), *"Muses Watering Pegasus,"* mark: WEDGWOOD, late 19th century, 8.25" h. . *Courtesy of Skinner, Inc., Boston and Bolton, Ma.* $1500-1800.

Vase, tricolor (solid, white with sage green and lilac relief), mark: WEDGWOOD, late 19th century, 3.625" h. *Courtesy of Skinner, Inc., Boston and Bolton, Ma.* $600-800.

Vase, dark blue (dip), *"Apollo Musagetes,"* mark: WEDGWOOD, ENGLAND, ca. 1900, 6.75" x 4". *Author's Collection.* $600-700.

Bud Vase, dark blue (dip, with lion heads), *"Sacrifice to Peace,"* mark: WEDGWOOD, ENGLAND, ca. 1900, 7" x 3". *Anonymous Private Collection.* $500-600.

Vase on Pedestal, pale blue (dip), unmarked but attributed to Wedgwood, ca. 1928, 18.5" x 7.5". *Courtesy of Jeffrey S. Milkins.* $1500-2000.

Bud Vase, dark blue (dip), *"Cupids as Seasons,"* mark: WEDGWOOD, ENGLAND, ca. 1900, 5.25" x 3". *Author's Collection.* $200-300

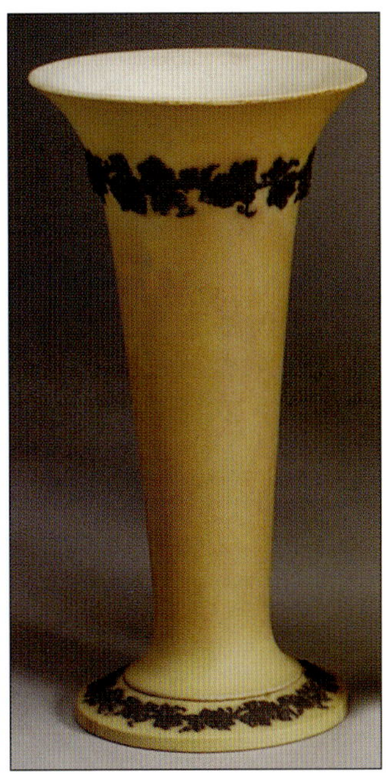

Vase, yellow buff (dip, with black relief), mark: WEDGWOOD, MADE IN ENGLAND, ca. 1930, 9.5" h. *Courtesy of Skinner, Inc., Boston and Bolton, Ma.* $600-800.

w. Odds and Ends

This ill-assorted group of Wedgwood Jasper items basically consists of pieces that could not be classified among the larger categories previously shown. All are very functional types and range in time from the eighteenth century to recent applications combining Wedgwood craftsmanship with modern technology.

Barometer, lilac (solid), *"Aurora,"* mark: WEDGWOOD, MADE IN ENGLAND, 1961, 9" diameter. *Courtesy of the Buten Collection of Wedgwood at the Sands Point Preserve, Sands Point, N.Y.* $400-500.

Bell Pull, diceware (dip, sage green with yellow quatrefoils), mark: not visible, ca. 1790, 2.5" x 1.25". *Courtesy of the Buten Collection of Wedgwood at the Sands Point Preserve, Sands Point, N.Y.* $1000-1200.

Pair of Bell Pulls, pale blue and white (solid), mark: none visible, ca. 1810, 2.5" x 1.25". *Courtesy of Drs. Elaine and Jeffrey Tulman.* $800-1000.

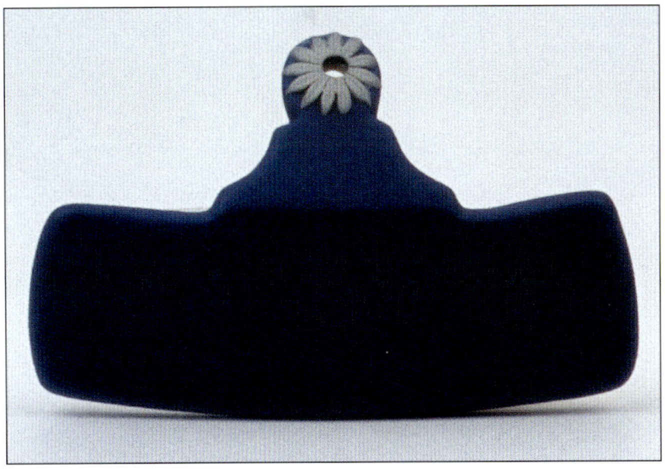

Botanical Garden Marker, dark blue (dip), mark: WEDGWOOD, ca. 1790, 0.5" x 1.25". *Courtesy of Dr. and Mrs. Victor Polikoff*. $400-500.

Pair of Buckle Plaques, tricolor (dip, dark blue and lilac), *"Hygeia" and "Venus and Cupid,"* mark: WEDGWOOD, early 19th century, 2.5" x 1.75". *Courtesy of Skinner, Inc., Boston and Bolton, Ma.* $1500-1800.

Buttons, dark blue (dip), mark: none visible, ca. 1790, 1" diameter, *Courtesy of Edward L. Knowles.* $900-1100.

Candle Snuffer and Stand, dark blue (dip), mark: WEDGWOOD, ca. 1890, 3.25" x 4". *Anonymous Private Collection.* $400-500.

Door Plate, sage green (dip), *"Terpsichore,"* mark: WEDGWOOD, ca. 1890, 8" x 2.5". *Courtesy of David Kroun.* $600-700.

Doorbell, pale blue (solid), mark: none visible, ca. 1955, 2.75" diameter, *Courtesy of Jeffrey S. Milkins.* $150-250.

Drum Base, tricolor (dip, dark blue and lilac), *"Cupid as Summer,"* mark: WEDGWOOD, early 19th century, 4.375". *Courtesy of Skinner, Inc., Boston and Bolton, Ma.* $1000-1200.

Keg Pump Handle, dark blue (dip), mark: none visible, ca. 1880, 6" x 2". *Courtesy of Adele Ierubino Barnett.* $300-400.

Drum Base, tricolor (dip, dark blue and yellow), *"Erato,"* mark: WEDGWOOD, early 19th century, 4.5". *Courtesy of Skinner, Inc., Boston and Bolton, Ma.* $1000-1200.

Monocular Case, dark blue (dip), *"Aesculapius and Hygeia,"* mark: non visible, ca. 1790 2" x 1.25". *Courtesy of Dr. and Mrs. Victor Polikoff.* $1000-1200.

Telephone, pale blue (solid), *"Sacrifice Figures,"* mark: WEDGWOOD, MADE IN ENGLAND, ca. 1965, 7.5" x 7". *Courtesy of Elizabeth and Paul Lauer.* $400-600.

Water Filter, pale blue (dip), *"Psyche Bound to a Tree by Cupids,"* marks: WEDGWOOD and Spencer's Patent Magnetic Purifying Filter, ca. 1890, 21" h. *Courtesy of Skinner, Inc., Boston and Bolton, Ma.* $2000-3000.

Writing Desk, five plaques (pale blue, mounted on ormolu), *"Dancing Hours,"* etc., marks: not visible, late 19th century, 11.5" w. *Courtesy of Skinner, Inc., Boston and Bolton, Ma.* $1800-2000.

Bibliography

Works about Wedgwood

Adams, Elizabeth Bryding. *The Dwight and Lucille Beeson Wedgwood Collection at the Birmingham Museum of Art.* Birmingham, Alabama: Birmingham Museum of Art: 1992.

Barnard, Harry. *Wedgwood Ware* (1924; reprint, East Ardsley, Yorkshire, England: EP Publishing Ltd., 1973).

Bedford, John. *Wedgwood Jasper Ware.* New York: Walker and Co., 1965

Book of Wedgwood Bas-reliefs, The. Barlaston Staffordshire, England: Josiah Wedgwood & Sons, Ltd., n.d.

Buten, David and Patricia Pelehach. *Wedgwood in America: Wedgwood Bas-Relief Ware.* Monographs in Wedgwood Studies, nos. 1 and 2. Merion, Pennsylvania: Buten Museum of Wedgwood, 1977.

Buten, Harry M. *Wedgwood ABC but not middle E.* Merion, Pennsylvania: Buten Museum of Wedgwood, 1964.

Dawson, Aileen. *Masterpieces of Wedgwood in the British Museum.* London: British Museum Publications, 1984.

Dolan, Brian. *Wedgwood, The First Tycoon.* New York: Viking Penguin, 2004.

Gorely, Jean. *Wedgwood.* New York: Gramercy Publishing Co., 1950.

Herman, Michael. *Wedgwood Jasper Ware, A Shape Book and Collectors Guide.* Atglen, Pennsylvania: Schiffer, 2003.

Meteyard, Eliza. *Wedgwood Trio by Meteyard.* Merion, Pennsylvania: Buten Museum of Wedgwood, 1967 (reprints in one volume of the author's *Wedgwood and His Works,* 1873, *Memorials of Wedgwood,* 1874 and *Choice Examples of Wedgwood Art,* 1879).

Rathbone, Frederick. *Old Wedgwood* (1898; reprint, Merion, Pennsylvania: Buten Museum of Wedgwood, 1968).

Reilly, Robin. *Wedgwood Jasper.* New York: Thames & Hudson, 1994.

_____. *Wedgwood, The New Illustrated Dictionary.* Woodbridge, Suffolk, England: The Collector's Club: 1995.

"The Story of Jasper: Part I – The 18th Century." *Etruria* , Vol. 3, No. 4 (Summer, 2000), pp. 17-20.

"The Story of Jasper: Part II – The 19th Century." *Etruria* , Vol. 4, No. 1 (undated), pp. 8-11.

"The Story of Jasper: Part III– Into the 20th Century." *Etruria* , Vol. 4, No. 2 (undated), pp. 8-10.

"The Story of Jasper: Part IV." *Etruria* , Vol. 4, No. 4 (undated), pp. 6-10.

Wills, Geoffrey. *Wedgwood.* London: Spring Books, 1988.

Josiah Wedgwood & Sons, Ltd., Barlaston, Stoke on Trent – Unpublished Material

Bas-Relief Ware, c.1920 (Mounting Ware Photos)

Catalogue of Bodies, Glazes and Shapes Current for 1940-1950

Price Book – 1924

Shape Book, First ,1802

Shape Book,1906-1913

Shape Book, 1913-1922

Shape Book, 1922-1929

Works about Classical Mythology

Grant, Michael and John Hazel. *Who's Who in Classical Mythology.* New York: Oxford University Press.

Graves, Robert. *The Greek Myths.* New York: Penguin USA, 1993.

Grimal, Pierre. *Dictionary of Classical Mythology.* Oxford, England: Blackwell Publishers, 1996.

Hamilton, Edith. *Mythology.* New York: Warner Books, 1942.

Index